# LIVING SYSTEM –
## Making sense of sustainability

For a complete list of Management Books 2000 titles,
visit our website on http://www.mb2000.com

# LIVING SYSTEM – Making sense of sustainability

## *Bruce Nixon*

### *Author of:*

*Making a Difference – Strategies and Tools for Transforming Your Organisation,* 2001, Management Books 2000, first published 1998 in hardback by Gilmour Drummond in UK and USA.

*Global Forces – a Guide for Enlightened Leaders – what Companies and Individuals Can Do,* 2000, updated 2003, Management Books 2000.

Cover painting by Jeanine de Waele

# Dedication

This book is dedicated to my family, Suzanne, Mark, Guy, Charlie, Hannah, George, grandsons, Orlando and Sholto, their descendants and everyone who reads it.

First published in 2006 by Management Books 2000 Ltd
Forge House, Limes Road
Kemble, Cirencester
Gloucestershire, GL7 6AD, UK
Tel:  0044 (0) 1285 771441
Fax: 0044 (0) 1285 771055
E-mail: info@mb2000.com
Web: www.mb2000.com

Printed and bound in Great Britain by 4edge Ltd of Hockley, Essex – www.4edge.co.uk

This book and the cover are printed on Cyclus papers, which are entirely recycled.

British Library Cataloguing in Publication Data is available
ISBN 1-85252-519-3

# Contents

# About the author

**As we get older,** we better understand what shaped us. I was brought up in the relatively affluent Wirral peninsula, Merseyside, by parents from Surrey and rural Gloucestershire.

**My childhood** was a time of caterpillars in nettles, willow herb, hedges and poplar trees, butterflies and moths, ponds and streams, frogs and newts, old steam engines and Crossville buses, electric trains, walking dogs in the countryside, swimming and sailing, mountain walking and cycling in Wales, Cheshire and down to Lands End, and, for ever reading, lying on Caldy Shore or Hilbre Island, surrounded by sea and sky.

**Earliest memories** made deep impressions: my father, partially disabled at the Somme, a piece of shrapnel in his head, saying he never wished to be an officer leading men to their deaths, with his allotment and hens, supplying money to ships, fire-watching at night on the roof of his Liverpool office; my mother, a single parent until she met him, widowed by the early death of her handsome Bessemer husband, who died painfully of TB years after being gassed in WW1 – as a little boy I could not understand why she still wept after marrying my father; WW1 war memorial on the hill, from which one night we saw Liverpool burning; a broken Dornier displayed in Liverpool amidst the ruins; shrapnel in the road; a lone Spitfire flying low over the sands; a bloated ship's dog, tea chests and oranges washed up on the shore; sunken ships in the channel; much older half brother, only survivor of his bomber crew who once ate at our house, and half sister, in the Land Army.

**Six months of law was too much.** Luckily, I got out to read philosophy, politics and economics at Oxford. Wirral was boring for a young person: off to London, continental Europe, Los Angeles, London, a long stay in Jamaica which deeply influenced me, visits to USA, back to London and a long visit to Canada. My career continued in corporate HR, management and organisation development and internal consulting. Then I started my consulting and writing business. Now, having become a minor activist, I spend more time writing, do occasional consulting and business school work.

**I am passionate about** sustainability and global justice – seeds sown doing history in the Birkenhead School Sixth and in Jamaica, where I lived and worked for nearly six years. This new book is the result. I love mountain walking, tropical fruit trees, vegetables, flowers, fragrant shrubs, organic cultivation, gardens, interior design and architecture, music, different cultures and hot countries, especially Southern Europe including Andalusia, Cuba, Mexico and above all Jamaica. Next stop India.

**I am a member** of the Association of Sustainability Practitioners, the Sustainable Development Network, Royal Society of Arts' Living Systems Group and, until recently, was on Council of the Association of Management Education and Development, now Hon member.

**I started writing** in 1980 and have published many articles. This is my fourth book.

# Thanks

Thanks to: my parents for their love and good influence; my diverse, pioneering, quirky ancestors; Suzanne, my wife, for her patience with me and hard work as one of my best editors and supporters; my children and grandchildren for educating me; my septuagenarian Christian head teacher,

Arthur Watts, founder of Kingsmead prep school; my sixth form History teacher Arthur Green – revolutions fascinated me – at Birkenhead School, there because luckily I failed my 11 plus; George Allen, my economics tutor at St Edmund Hall, Oxford.

Dr Keith Panton, ex CEO and Chairman of Alcan Jamaica and consultant Ilsa DuVerney have inspired me and got me back to Jamaica three times so far.

*Kingsmead School*

People who have helped transform my thinking include: Meg Wheatley, Fritjof Capra, Dr Vandana Shiva, Barry Coates, former Director of WDN, now Executive Director, Oxfam New Zealand, Eileen Conn, John Field and other colleagues in the Royal Society of Arts Living Systems Group, Esther Roycroft-Boswell who co-led HDRA's first study tour of organic cultivation in Cuba, Francesca Romana Giordano, Herbert Giradet, John Bunzl, James Robertson, Jean Woollard, John Hawken, John Jopling, John Noble, Mary Jo Radcliffe, Mary Thompson, Matti Kohonen, Dr Mike Munro Turner, Dr Neslyn Watson-Druée, MBE, Canon Peter Challen, Peter Critten, Robin Coates, Rodney Shakespeare, Roy Madron, Susan Dye and Tarek El Diwany. 10 years ago, I was profoundly influenced by three wise women and Satish Kumar at the Schumacher College.

To ... Mike and Liz Zeidler, through whom I joined the especially fruitful Association of Sustainability Practitioners, recently formed with Anita Roddick's support; similarly, Penny Walker and Jim Hopwood, for the Sustainable Development Network; Gilmour Drummond, my first publisher, and my present publisher James Alexander: creative, flexible, supportive, cheerful, funny, good-hearted, practical and with a quick intelligence quite unlike mine. How could I have managed without him? Lorraine Waumsley, Sustainability consultant and educator, has helped me with information, ideas and editing. Those I omit, please excuse me.

# Acknowledgements

**Conjuring uniqueness**
This book, though unique, is not original – very little is. I discovered years ago that my core process is *'conjuring uniqueness.'* So it embraces many original people and their ideas. I have tried conscientiously to acknowledge as many as possible. You can easily locate these through **Resources and References** at the back of the book. I acknowledge BBC's World Service; many TV and radio programmes; many websites here and overseas including those of the BBC, Independent and Guardian and Google. The copyrights of painters, Jeanine de Waele, who provided the cover picture, and Rosalind Bendix-Lewis are acknowledged.

Photographs: Old oak tree and market in Alamos, Mexico by Guy Nixon; African village by Zareh Nercessian, California; Welsh Assembly building by Alex Skibinski, Cardiff. Remainder by author and other family members.

# Foreword from the USA

**From Margaret Wheatley**

## It's Just Our Turn to Help the World

Several years ago, I read of a Buddhist teacher who offered his encouragement to a group that was filled with despair over the state of the world. His advice was simple, profound and placed things in historical context: *'It's just our turn to help the world.'* What I love about this statement is that it reminds us of other times and other people who stepped forward to help create the changes that were necessary. We do live in an extraordinary era when, for the first time, humans have altered the planet's ecology and created consequences which are just beginning to materialise in frightening ways. But throughout human existence, there have always been people willing to step forward to struggle valiantly in the hope that they might reverse the downward course of events. Some succeeded, some did not. But as we face our own time, we need to remember that we stand on very firm and solid shoulders.

In my own work with local communities around the planet, I've learned to define leadership quite differently than the norm. A leader is anyone willing to help, anyone who sees something that needs to change and takes the first steps to influence that situation. It might be a parent who intervenes in her child's school; or a group in a rural village in Africa who decides to put in a well for fresh water; or a worker who refuses to allow mistreatment of others in his workplace; or an individual who rallies his or her neighbors to stop local polluters. Everywhere in the world, no matter the economic or social circumstances, I see people stepping forward to make a small difference. They are impelled to act in spite of themselves; they often describe their actions as 'I couldn't not do it.' Others see what they do and label them as courageous, but those who step forward never feel courageous. They just did what felt like the right thing to do.

Because a leader is anyone willing to help, we can celebrate the fact that the world has an abundance of leaders. Some people ask, 'where have all the good leaders gone?' But when we worry that there's a deficit of leaders, we're just looking in the wrong place. We need to look locally. And we need to look at ourselves. Where have we been willing to step forward for the issues that we care about?

Every great change initiative in the world begins with the actions of just a few people. Even those that win the Nobel Peace Prize. I've looked at the history of several of these prize-winning efforts, and one phrase always pops up as the founders describe how they began. Their laudable efforts began not with plans and official permission, but when 'some friends and I started talking.' I recently listened to Wangari Matai, winner of the 2005 Nobel Peace Prize for her work in planting over 30 million trees in Kenya and east Africa. Her first efforts were with a few local women, and they planted seven trees, five of which died. But they learned from that experience, spread the learning to their villages, then to other networks, and ten years later, 30 million trees flourish. Villages now have clean water and local firewood, creating improved health and community vitality. And it all began 'when some friends and I started talking.'

Bruce has compiled many similar wonderful stories in this provocative and stirring book. Individuals have an idea, or experience a tragedy, or want to resolve an injustice, and they step forward to help. Instead of being overwhelmed and withdrawing, as many of us do these days, here are people who decided to act locally. They didn't know at the beginning where it would end up. They didn't spend a great deal of time planning and getting official support. They began, they learned from their mistakes, they kept going. They followed the energy of yes rather than accepting defeat. This is how the world always changes. And this is how we must act now to respond to the frightening issues of these times, to reverse our direction, to restore hope to the future.

I carry with me a vision of what would be possible if more and more of us were willing to help, if we simply said 'no' to what disturbs us, if we took a stand, if we refused to be cowed or silenced. My heroes are the Ukrainians. They set a standard in their 'Orange Revolution' in late 2004 that has now inspired citizens in many different countries as far flung as Ecuador and Nepal. They refused to give in or to stop protesting until they got what they needed. Why couldn't we do the same? What will be our response to the destructive behaviors, the injustices and the suicidal decisions and beliefs that Bruce so well-details in this book? Are we willing to help?

### I Want to Be a Ukrainian      Meg Wheatley ©2005

> When I come of age,
> When I get over being a teenager,
> When I take my life seriously
> When I grow up
>    I want to be a Ukrainian.
> When I come of age
> I want to stand happily in the cold
> for days beyond number,
> no longer numb to what I need.
>    I want to hear my voice
>    rise loud and clear above
>    the icy fog, claiming myself.

It was day fifteen of the protest, and a woman standing next to her car was being interviewed. Her car had a rooster sitting on top of it. She said, *'We've woken up and we're not leaving till this rotten government is out.'* It is not recorded if the rooster crowed.

> *When I get over being a teen-ager*
> *when I no longer complain or accuse*
> *when I stop blaming everybody else*
> *when I take responsibility*
> *I will have become a Ukrainian*

The Yushchenko supporters carried bright orange banners which they waved vigorously on slim poles. Soon after the protests began, the government sent in thugs hoping to create violence. They also carried banners, but theirs were hung on heavy clubs that could double as weapons.

> *When I take my life seriously*
> *when I look directly at what's going on*
> *when I know that the future doesn't change itself*
> *that I must act*
> *I will be a Ukrainian.*

'Protest that endures,' Wendell Berry said, 'is moved by a hope far more modest than that of public success: namely, the hope of preserving qualities in one's own heart and spirit that would be destroyed by acquiescence.

> *When I grow up and am known as a Ukrainian*
> *I will move easily onto the streets*
> *confident, insistent, happy to preserve the qualities*
> *of my own heart and spirit.*
> *In my maturity, I will be glad to teach you*
> *the cost of acquiescence*
> *the price of silence*
> *the peril of retreat.*

'Hope,' said Vaclav Havel, 'is not the conviction that something will turn out well, but the certainty that something makes sense regardless of how it turns out.'

> *I will teach you all that I have learned*
> *the strength of fearlessness*
> *the peace of conviction*
> *the strange source of hope*
> *and I will die well, having been a Ukrainian.*

**Margaret Wheatley, Ed.D, Utah, USA. ©2006**
*Margaret Wheatley writes, teaches, and speaks about radically new practices and ideas for organising in chaotic times.*

# Foreword from the UK

## From Dame Anita Roddick

**This book is about sustainability in the broadest sense** – the environment, the ecological system on which all life depends, global social and economic justice and the need for respect for all difference amongst human beings and in nature. It calls for a change in values and consciousness that will not only save the planet but put an end to violence. It calls for an end to mono thinking, monoculture and the habits of domination, imperialism and attempting to colonise thought as well as cultures and nations.

**The uniqueness of the book.** It advocates understanding and addressing *the underlying system and the values beneath it* as the best way forward if we are to realise our hopes for a fair and sustainable World. The system Bruce describes is a living system embracing all human beings and the Earth they live in.

**Living systems always react if not respected.** We are part of a living system – each of us here for but an instant in time. So we owe if to our children and descendants to be good stewards and act wisely. This is what leaders must learn or they are a danger. Once you understand it you see it everywhere, every day. This is what we have been confronted with particularly from the beginning of the 21st Century. The tragedies and catastrophes are warnings – 9/11 and its successors, global terrorism, violence, climate change and destruction of the ecosystem. We need to learn from them or there will be much worse to come. Poverty, lack of respect, injustice, greed and domination are at the root of it. Current beliefs in 'Western' leadership have only made things worse – more poverty and violence – not less. We have to face the truth. We delude ourselves with slogans, blatantly misleading words.

**The key elements of the system** are an uncritical belief in global sourcing and 'science', domination of nature, domination by global and regional institutions by business, which also undermines 'democracy', racist foreign policies, untruthfulness and denial, destabilising financial markets, the money debt system, perverse taxation, tax evasion and distortion of the purpose of business and responsibilities of directors.

**Underlying the system** is the dominant value of putting money and power before meeting human needs, unconscious racism and an imbalance of male and female energies.

Bruce puts forward *a new agenda for the 21st Century* to address these issues including a renewable Charter for big companies and citizen's basic income.

**Whilst radical, it is also realistic** and respectful of other views. It ranges from strategic issues and proposals to down to earth practical steps anyone can take. It takes a historical and spiritual perspective attempting to learn from History. It is very balanced in tone and content recognising the positive contributions, the up side and the down or dark side; challenging, hopeful, encouraging and appreciating. Bruce believes in seeing the good in people, putting attention on good models, what works and finding common ground – rather than verbal or physical violence which has been increasingly used by the 'West' on a massive scale.

**There are amazing revelations** in the research he draws on e.g. war and foreign policy and his study of politics in our parliament – the *'Mother of Parliamentary Democracy'*.

Of particular interest are the ideas about **sustainable buildings and cities** and the notion that they belong to people, who need to be involved in the co-creation of important buildings and town and cityscapes. Our environment is essential to mental and emotional health and communities that work for people of all ages and incomes. There are some valuable positive examples.

Bruce believes we are all **mirrors of each other** and if we are to change things for the better we need to look first inside ourselves – including acknowledging *the beast within us all*. We need to be truthful, show respect and build partnership based on trust and good relationships.

He believes we have **much to learn from wise women**, who may save us from ourselves. There are many wise women in this book.

**Dame Anita Roddick, England**

# Why this book?

## A people's book

**We are approaching disaster**. Sustainability includes both environmental degradation and global economic injustice because both are creating an unsustainable world. Why are we so slow to change, when the situation is so threatening and there is worse news every day? Why do we not learn from history? With all the information we have, why aren't we taking sustainability more seriously? It has taken Suzanne and me two years to sign up for Ecotricity!   Why don't more companies fully embrace the Chairman of Interface, Ray Anderson's philosophy of 'do well by doing good' making sustainability central, at the heart of their business? Why is Government so slow and not joined up, different departments pulling in opposite directions?

**I believe in seeing the good in people.**  Most directors, managers and employees are good people trying to provide good products and services and create a good workplace where people enjoy coming to work and can give their best. They are trying to be good parents, family members, neighbours and community members; they care about the kind of world we are creating for ourselves, and future generations.

### So what gets in the way?
More and more these questions have preoccupied me.

This new book is the result.

**Making sense of it all.** The book is an attempt to do just that. If we want to change things for the better we first need to understand the underlying system. Part of making sense is seeing the underlying patterns that present themselves every day, seeing the world as a *living system*. In a living system there are always actions and reactions. It is a picture of chaos, contradictions and opposites because that is how we are and how a living system is. That will be a constant theme in the book. We are partners in the living system.

*Once you understand the living system, you will see it every day.*

The key thing to understand is: living systems hit back harshly if not respected.  That is what is happening – warning us that problem solving and expensive 'fixes' do not work. We need a fundamental change to resolve the big issues of our time by transforming the underlying economic model and the values beneath it. We need a change in consciousness, which means change within ourselves.

*Leaders who do not understand this are a danger.*

**Transformation partly takes place through big shifts and unique individuals.** It also comes about through millions of people taking all kinds of actions. I provide information about many ways in which people are making benign changes and suggest how you can act to improve the situation – putting pressure on political and business leaders, joining with other people, starting a new enterprise, exercising leadership, creative initiatives in your work whatever it is, in your community and family and by making changes in your own life and the way you live.

This is a *'people's book,'* easy to read, a contribution to this process.

**I want it to shock and challenge people** as I have been shocked and challenged in writing this book.

*'Shake me up, Judy.'*

Bleak House, Charles Dickens

But, I want **to focus on the positive**, giving inspiration and hope.

*'Everything that is done in the world is done by hope.'*

Martin Luther King

**What this book is and is not.** It's about *systemic change.* It does not offer expertise about the steps needed to bring about a sustainable future. There are excellent books, by experts, on saving the planet, and how you can do that; some are listed in the resources section.

Articles, processes, books reviews, my other books, information, resources and services are available in ***Creating better workplaces for the 21st Century*** at www.brucenixon.com. I welcome feedback through this website or otherwise.

# Prologue

## The world has changed ... and so have I

**The world has changed dramatically**, since my two previous books were published in 2000 and 2001. A living system does.

*We are now far more aware of the environmental emergency, whatever its causes, global economic and social injustice and the dangerous gap between people everywhere.*

A big difficulty about writing a book like this is that the world changes every day, sometimes dramatically. I struggle, as I write, to keep up with it. It is difficult to stop, as thoughts keep coming and exciting new things, many wonderful and positive, arrive at my 'door'. However...

*What matters is seeing the patterns.*

**Sometimes we need to be shocked.** Above all, the horrifying and tragic 9/11 suicide attack was a turning point, followed by the 'war on terror' in Afghanistan, 'regime change' in Iraq, and the resistance, counter attacks of 'insurgents' who may see themselves as 'resistance' – think of Europe in WW2 – more attacks in Madrid, Egypt, Bali, Jordan, Israel, London's 7/7 and Palestine. Suicide bombings, the reach of international terrorism and the threat of nuclear terrorism make it clear that no nation is safe, however powerful. These shocking and terrible personal tragedies compare with the horrors, wasted lives, disease, so-called 'natural disasters' that result from poverty in poor and rich countries and the civil wars, also mostly in poor countries. Road 'accidents' – so called – are often sheer irresponsibility or criminality.

*Words are important in scrutinising truth.*

Corporate scandals have revealed the scale of corruption at the top of big business and increased distrust of corporations. Corporate Responsibility and Business Interruption are higher on the agenda as a result. Progress is undermined by the lack of a level playing field. Gordon Brown's sudden scrapping of new rules for Corporate Operating and Financial Reviews has not helped.

Similar patterns emerge in politics. All this reflects the human psyche within all of us.

**It is clear we face an emergency.** The human contribution to climate change has been recognised by all but a tiny, powerful minority. Melting ice caps, rising seas, increasing instability of our weather, drought, loss of species and their migrations north have presented us with overwhelming evidence (World Energy Outlook report, International Energy Agency). Unfortunately, that tiny minority includes George Bush, and his colleagues, who represent the biggest polluting and most powerful nation. They should be giving far-sighted 21st Century leadership as *part of* the rest of the world, having learned the lessons of history. Even the disaster in New Orleans has not convinced them. Politicians have a long record of suppressing inconvenient information. Many of his people are far ahead of him and losing patience. Slowly 'turning,' Bush is beginning to say most surprising things for an oilman

**Poverty, global social and economic injustice, are higher up the agenda too.** The problems are no longer somewhere else. Our inter-connectedness and the implications of global sourcing are demonstrated by the current threat of Avian flu and the surging flow of migrants seeking a better life or fleeing oppression. We are a part of these problems – our economic and foreign policies have helped create them – the plight of Africa, the victims of tsunami, the continuing consequences of earthquakes in Kashmir, hurricane Katrina in New Orleans and land falls in Guatemala. Floods in Mumbai in 2005 were worse than ever before, followed by an outbreak of Leptospirosis, shocking at the time, soon forgotten, like Jamaica. The poor are always hardest hit. New Orleans brought renewed attention to the depth of poverty and injustice in the richest country in the world. Numerous campaigns like Sir Bob Geldof's Live 8 concerts and Make Poverty History shake things up. But G8 meetings produce numerous statements of commitment but, as before, not much delivery. Progress is desperately slow and mostly not on the right basis.

As Desmond Tutu says, kindly, *'there is room for considerable improvement'*!

**Information is not the issue – it's making sense of it all and acting.** We now know enough. Google gives access to massive resources of information, a godsend to authors like me. There are hundreds of NGOs and internet newsletters to subscribe to. Deluged with information in the media and especially through the internet, we have 'information overload' as Alvin Toffler predicted 30 years ago.

It's standing back, seeing the patterns, getting a sense of urgency, outrage and anger, using that energise us into taking bold action that will make deep change happen. Ordinary people, like you and me, have far more power than we realise.

**We need to create deeply felt awareness, a change of consciousness and, above all, hope.** I believe we are on the brink of massive change. All the horrors and tragedies of the past few years have helped bring this about. We are at a turning point – if we choose to be!

**I have changed,** grown older and more radical, as one does. Time seems short. I am willing to speak my mind and take a stand! Since writing my previous two books, I have learned a lot I want to share with you, particularly the key role of abusing nature and **debt money in driving *unsustainability*.**

**Personal sustainability** is equally important. Otherwise I am not living the change I want to see. Writing *Global Forces* in 2000, and revising it after 9/11, was difficult. At night I woke up, writing in my head, listening to the BBC World Service and in the early morning, *Farming Today, Open Country, Living World* and *Something Understood*. The research exhausted me. Afterwards, I went walking in the Sierra Nevada to restore myself. I am trying to write *sustainably* this time. Until now, I tried to get everything done as well as possible, as fast as possible, attempting to do several other things, often driving everyone around me mad, and myself, neglecting loved ones and me.

**Mindfulness.** This time I wanted to write with 'mindfulness' – being in the 'now', enjoying the experience rather than getting the book written. That's what we need to do in all work. (There's a good explanation of mindfulness in Thich Nhat Hanh's book, *The Miracle of Mindfulness*.) I have been trying to do 'one thing at a time' and listening to music, taking the advice of Stephan Solzhenitsyn, son of Aleksandr: *'The easiest way to calm down was to play Bach.'* (BBC R4).

**This book is intended to be an easier write; an easy read** – you will judge the latter. I have enjoyed the writing more. My new attitude has helped – so has the relative ease of researching via the internet – though easy to get gross 'information over-load.' Sometimes what I read shocks me.

**Making sense.** Writing helps me make sense of it all too! I do not need to research so much. In a strange way, what I need just 'walks in through the door.' I feel not in control. It is a much bigger challenge than I expected. I am surprised by what I have written, as if the book writes through me. Ironically, trying to make sense of globalisation, makes sense of writing a book and makes sense of me. The book is chaotic, reflecting the chaotic nature of the living system it describes – not a misleadingly tidy picture of our world.

**'Ordinary' people change the world** – another lesson I've re-learnt – not for the most part big leaders or big institutions – except before they get big. Often 'going with the flow,' working with the energy, works better than battering at ramparts. Yet sometimes we have to! As institutions grow bigger they tend to become rigid, focussed internally on vested interests, power and maintaining hierarchy. Unconsciously, they are about defence, denial, 'group think', steady state and keeping things essentially the way they are. Their leaders have often become out of touch with ordinary lives; do not understand how to create good workplaces, how to lead or bring about change in the 21st Century.

Leaders like this need to be challenged and pushed by 'ordinary' people like you and me.

**This book is particularly for you, everyone who cares** about the situation and wants to make a difference in some way. It will be unpredictably out of date tomorrow. That doesn't matter much. Patterns and the underlying system continue – unless we change them. Human nature, which we have to understand, changes imperceptibly – why else are Shakespeare, Dickens and the Romantics still so relevant to understanding ourselves?

I keep remembering both:

> *'Whatever you do may seem insignificant,*
> *but it is most important that you do it.'*

Mahatma Gandhi

And, the Samurai image of man as:

> *'a leaf floating on the river of life.'*

**Bruce Nixon, Berkhamsted, 2nd June, 2006**

*'Cornfield' by Rosalyn Bendix-Lewis*

## Chapter 1

# The Wonderful World at the Beginning of the 21st Century

> This chapter, like all the others is inevitably written from a mainly 'Western', and European, perspective. The whole book is full of contradictions and opposites like 'up side' and a 'down side', hope and despair. There always are both and it is hard to keep them apart. That applies to most chapters including this.

**It's a wonderful world, full of opportunity and possibilities.** Life is a miracle. Life is energy. On balance things get better. Human beings generally want good things for other human beings. We like to make things better, more beautiful and more harmonious. The prevailing creative energy is love – love for each other, love for one's place and work, love for the planet, all its wonder and mystery, all its creatures, our healing relationships with cat or dog, and other forms of life. Pictures of the Earth from space enabled us to see our small planet for the first time and the wonder of it all. Looking down on our countries from a plane we see great beauty. A sense of wonder and mystery grows as science and technology reveal more about the brain in our bodies and the whole universe. Thousands of NGOs, working for a better world, are an expression of love. It is our distress, hopelessness, lack of respect, and the way we have been damaged that get in our way. Things get better all the time, especially when we listen with compassion to others' hopes and feelings and we behave as fellow human beings. Then prejudices and fears dissolve; we realise what it is to be human; that we are all basically the same, not alone.

*Sierra Nevada*

**Travelling easily,** cheaply and safely gives us a greater appreciation of the wonder, rich diversity and beauty of the planet and the man-made world. It helps us build friendships across the world and with people of different cultures, often living simpler lives. But air travel pollutes the atmosphere with $CO_2$ and contributes to global warming.

**The 'West' is a freer, far more exciting place than 50 years ago** when I was a young person. For many people, especially in the 'West,' life has improved immeasurably compared with a few generations ago. We have choice and opportunity as never before – that requires more responsibility. Capitalism has had amazing successes. Our present day democracies, for all their flaws, work better than dictatorship.

**The human story is of major technological innovations,** every few hundred years, transforming how we live. Microsoft's benign mission *'to enable people and businesses throughout the world to realise their full potential'* is working.

**It is also the story of many bottom-up revolutions** – like Rosa Parks' brave refusal to give up her bus seat to a white, which sparked off the civil rights revolution in USA and our own Maya Anne Evans of Justice Not Vengeance, who was recently arrested near Downing Street for reading out the names of the British soldiers killed in Iraq.

**It truly is a connected world.** We connect with each other in ways not possible even five or so years ago.

**Using his cheap mobile card**, our 19-year-old son talks with us almost daily, sounds of Brooklyn or Manhattan in the background as he walks to Pace University campus. He does not seem so far away. Almost every morning before starting work, our daughter, at university in Norwich, and I exchange short emails, helping us start the day by laughing. The young Mozart and his anxious parents, nurturing his genius, did something similar as he travelled precariously and uncomfortably round Europe. Their exchanges took many days.

**Everywhere, people are talking more.** Conversation helps bring about change. Tyrants, knowingly, always try to stop it. A billion people now have mobile phones, transforming communications, especially in African countries, unable to afford expensive infrastructure. People run businesses from mobiles.

**The internet is enabling many conversations and empowering people.** In our thousands, we can now much more easily take action to change things for the better. Through the internet and Google, we have rapid access to more information and dialogue than ever before. It's almost impossible to keep people in ignorance. Digital television and radio – digital radio and the Podcast – at the computer – give 24 hour access to music and the bold BBC World Service, innumerable websites and campaigns. Blogs give access to new accounts of history, exposing things some people would prefer to keep hidden, forgotten. Websites are often interactive, inviting people to contribute their opinions, stories or photographs. They tell how to take action, invite them to sign petitions or send campaign cards or letters.

**It is easy to create campaigning websites**, join petitions and mass campaigns, lobby representatives in parliament, heads of government and government ministers.

UK TV Channel 4's **revolutionary campaign for X-listing bad buildings** (*Bad Buildings*) empowers people living with them, their spirits numbed by them. Presenter Kevin McCloud says that town centres do not belong to corporations, architects, planners and experts – *'they belong to people.'* 8,000 have already signed up including me.

**An explosion of citizen reporting is democratising the press.** 2005 has been the year of the digital citizen, claims Jo Twist (Institute for Public Policy Research) in BBC News – pictures of 7/7 and tsunami taken by mobiles. In the USA, the video blogger or vlogger emerges. Some predict vlogging will transform local and national elections. There is a growing appetite to be involved and shake up tardy institutions (Centre for Citizen Media).

If you want to know what the USA (please, not *'America,'* a huge diverse continent. Bush's words beguile!) is really like for ordinary people, how their democracy works, well and not so well, go to Google and put in your questions. It's interesting to contrast it with much maligned Cuba.

**There is growing freedom from tyranny and tyranny of the mind** – state and religious – but particularly tyrannies of the mind, that constrained what we dared to think and say. Television and the internet are exposing Europe's, and others' shameful pasts – like the Inquisition and Australia's persecution of Aboriginals (*Rabbit Proof Fence*).

Yet, **although technology can empower us** – complicating as it is – it may not make us happier. Unless used wisely, it makes for unhealthy, stressful lives; destroys the planet and its beauty; and creates widespread poverty in every sense.

**We enjoy, particularly in cosmopolitan cities, a wonderful diversity of people, cultures and religions.** London has been transformed for the better in the past ten years or so. We enjoy world music, film, clothing and food. My local supermarket is full of out of season and tropical fruit and vegetables – once unobtainable except in ethnic communities. In southern England, we have a more Mediterranean climate – sitting out on the street for coffee and meals, growing grapes, peaches, almond nuts and even tea. Coriander now grows in Yorkshire.

**More and more people benefit from complementary therapies**, saving them from severe disease before it starts or gets a hold – yoga, Tai Chi, Quigong, meditation, acupuncture and Ayurvedic medicine. Previous generations did not have this blessing. Western people are turning to African, Asian, Islamic Sufi, Muslim, Maori and Native American teachings. The Dalai Lama and Osho have benefited many people. We are learning from Buddhism, Hinduism and Tantra the sacredness of sexuality, different from the 'West's' unhealthy history of oppression, suppression, distortion, abuse, commercial exploitation that causes anguish about a source of creation and creativity. Sexuality is an energy force – hence its suppression in the past in case it would release revolution. We are becoming more emotionally, spiritually and sexually intelligent and respectful, something only a few of our parents enjoyed. Mozart's genius gave him an intuitive grasp of the complexity of the human psyche and Tantric energy to which his music connects us. Hence, his music excites our energy (BBC R3 *Desperately Seeking Mozart*).

There is growing reconciliation and respect for difference: other people's religions, 'minorities' (often global majorities – misleading words again!), women, young people, people of different sexual orientation – and appreciation of the importance of diversity in contributing to the most successful societies and preventing war. Britain's first black Archbishop, John Tucker Mugabi Sentamu (criticism of the Amin regime for its human rights violations led to his arrest and departure from Uganda to the UK) expresses values of *'justice, peace and love'*. Recently with Kofi Anan, he spoke out against Guantanamo Bay, urging Bush to close it. Anticipating next year's bicentenary of the Abolition of the Slave Trade Act of 1807, the Anglican Church Synod has issued an apology *'in the light of our involvement in the slave trade and of the Christian demands of repentance and sorrow'*. Chief Rabbi Sir Jonathan Sachs speaks of *'free speech and responsible speech.'* So called 'rottweiler', Pope Benedict, writes his first Encyclical on the importance of love.

For the first time, Bolivians have elected by a large majority an indigenous Aymaran President, Evo Morales. To the US government's discomfort, he praises Fidel Castro whilst Venezuelan President Hugo Chavez, describes Tony Blair, not so respectfully, as *'a pawn of imperialism'* (meaning George Bush). Latin America is going left. In the UK, gay couples have the right to form civil partnerships. Earlier this year, legislation in Scotland made it an offence to stop nursing mothers from feeding their babies in places like bars, buses and shopping centres.

**There is a growing understanding of the importance of respect, diversity and the dire consequences of the opposite.** Tolerance towards Christians and Jews was the secret of Muslim Spain's success in the 10th century. Caliph Al-Hakam II (961-976) founded a library of hundreds of thousands of volumes, practically inconceivable in Europe at that time.

When Europe was in the Dark Ages, Muslims brought their own and Greek and Roman civilisation to Spain. Their thinkers stood out, above all in medicine, mathematics and astronomy (Si Spain). A

*Seville*

few centuries later, Christopher Columbus, used maps created by Islamic scholars in Spain. Many innovations, now central to our lives, including coffee and roses came from the Islamic world. We learn from other cultures. Holocaust Memorial Day now honours more genocides than the 11million Jews killed by Nazis. Some point out the white, Euro-centric title needs to be changed to Genocide Memorial Day to signal the inclusion of genocides everywhere – including the Inquisition – committed by and against most religious groups and races throughout the centuries. These far exceed the estimated 38million battle-dead killed in 20th century, aside from earlier, international wars.

**The tragic violence of suicide bombing** is forcing us to learn more about what Islam really teaches, injustice in the Middle East and Muslim history and traditions. There's always a gift in tragedy – another example of how a living system works. Many Muslims and Christians realise the urgency of getting closer and understanding each other better. After Christians, Muslims are the second largest religious group in the world. It is heartening to read of Islamic Relief, Cafod and Christian Aid working alongside each other, bringing relief to earthquake victims in Pakistan. (Christian Aid News, *'Your god is my God'*)

**More women in leadership, give grounds for hope.** Mary Wollstonecraft, 1790s author of *'A Vindication of the Rights of Woman'*, who also opposed slavery, would be happier, but still 'in there' fighting. Women in the UK were chattels with no vote until the twenties. Now there are more women Ministers and MPs than in Margaret Thatcher's day, and at the top of business. However the culture of most boardrooms and the House of Commons is still male.

Germany has its first woman Chancellor, Angela Merkel. Helen Clark is New Zealand's PM. In Iran, a record 513 women stood in the February 2005 polls, making about 7% of candidates nationwide, and nearly 15% in the capital Tehran. Portia Simpson Miller is the first woman Jamaican Prime Minister and the second in the Caribbean! *'The fact that she is a woman is what is needed at this time. Wars and hardware, logic and so on, are what drive male thinking and approaches. A woman will bring understanding and compassion – something that is new to governance in Jamaica,'* said colleague Jennifer Edwards. Ellen Johnson-Sirleaf, known as the 'Iron Lady', first woman to be elected president of Liberia, or anywhere in Africa, with 91% of ballots, won 59% of the vote. A former World Bank economist, she is popular with women and the educated elite. Women pilots now fly BA jets to worldwide destinations like Hong Kong.

**Chile's just elected third woman President, Michelle Bachelet**, centre-left, 54-year old single mother of three, victim of junta torture when a 22-year old medical student, at her news conference pledged a cabinet with an equal number of men and said:

*'Because I was the victim of hatred, I have dedicated my life to reverse that hatred and turn it into understanding, tolerance and – why not say it – into love,' and 'to create a country which is more prosperous, more just, a country of greater solidarity.'*

Rival, conservative businessman Sebastian Pinera, congratulated her saying she represents,

*'The struggle of millions of women to reach the position they deserve'.*

On the **proposed Free Trade Area of the Americas**, she believes every country should be allowed to join at its own pace; she seeks reconciliation with neighbours and opposed the Iraq war (Her story of being tortured can be found on Google).

**Women are pushing the glass ceiling:** now more women than men millionaires aged 18 to 40. Often being more sensitive to relationships, mood and atmosphere, they can make better, more flexible and emotionally intelligent bosses than the usual man. Men are becoming more aware of their feminine and intuitive side. Women in the workforce have increased by one third since 1975; new fathers now spend far more time with their children. Controversy over women Bishops in the C of E is being resolved.

**There are always two forces at work** – the benign and the opposing belief, just as sincerely held and principled. I believe the 'benign' tendency prevails. Just as individuals are on a life journey towards wholeness, so is society (Chapter 7).

**Britain's Equal Opportunities Commission's warns** that sex equality laws need to be modernised to continue tackling discrimination. After 30 years, women are still sacked for being pregnant and their absence in most boardrooms is well known. The Women and Work Commission concludes that the gender pay gap is worse in Britain than anywhere in Europe. Women in full-time work were earning 17% less than men; their lifetime earnings for equivalent work and retirement incomes are far behind men's – in the financial sector, £1m less (*Shaping a Fairer Future*). It costs the British economy up to £23bn a year in lost productivity and wasted talent.

**Technological innovation**, shifting the 'industrial revolution' to Asia, gives many people in the 'West' freedom from harsh labour, the prospect of longer and healthier lives and cures undreamed of 50 years ago. However it transfers Victorian working conditions to many people, including women and children, in Asia and elsewhere.

**Diseases that killed millions in previous centuries** are all but eliminated or could be if funds were made available. Medical advances find new cures and simpler less invasive and less expensive operations facilitated by microsurgery, saving lives as well as money. Much more is to come in the relief of human suffering through the discovery of the human genome, and stem cell research may offer cures for such distressing conditions as Parkinson's disease and senile dementia. Money making and the 'celebrity surgeon', soon get in the way, though.

**New technology could cut serious car crashes** by 48% and deaths on the road by 59% by controlling irresponsible drivers who exceed speed limits, forcing us to adjust speed to the road conditions, reducing $CO_2$ emissions and saving our suspensions from humps.

**Intelligent Speed Adaption,** fitted to every car for road charging could warn us and put on the brakes when we exceed the speed limit or drive too fast. Despite UK having the best safety record in Europe, 3,508 people were killed and 33,707 gravely injured on UK roads in 2004, enough to fill 30 jumbo jets – all family tragedies. It will happen to 1 in 17 of us. In one week, more die on our roads than all our casualties in Iraq. The carnage since 1945 exceeds all deaths of British soldiers in WW2. Replicated throughout the world, most deaths and injuries are due to lunatic driving (George Montbiot, February, 2005, Road Peace's Safety First).

**It's a crazy, upside down world** when these road injuries and deaths attract far less attention than the equally tragic and horrifying 9/11 and suicide bombings – we have seen these events on TV screens; few of us have witnessed dead young people in a smashed car.

**Not enough money or effort goes into research into the environmental and dietary causes of diseases such as cancer.** In our crazy world, the money is to be made, not in promoting health and prevention, but in expensive, though extremely important, dis-ease curing: technology, pharmaceuticals, plastic surgery and helping women, desperate to conceive. If the goal is to reduce human suffering, health promotion and disease prevention deserve equal investment. In the long term, prevention will be much cheaper and better for everyone, except big 'polluters' and businesses profiting from unhealthy lifestyles. That work is under-funded, relatively poorly paid and earns less profit. Fertility experts become the medical profession's highest earners, making fortune's like Dr Mohamed Taranissl's £20m and Professor Ian Craft's £10m (as reported in the media). The market is not good at allocating funds to the highest priorities for society or rewarding people performing the greatest service to humanity. 'Compensation' is a funny word used by HR specialists. Is high pay compensation for doing relative harm?

**This, mostly positive picture, is an affluent 'Western' one** (unconscious racism again – e.g. USA is East on Japanese maps) from a minority world, largely out of touch with how most people on the planet live, in their own countries and in the so-called 'third world' (another racism). The downside again: prosperous we may be but often so hurried and stressed as to be out of touch with ourselves – our bodies, hearts and spirits and the healing beauty of nature.

**We have far too much whilst the most human beings have far too little.** It is driving us crazy.

Recently a friend sent me this extract from *The End of Growth: Efforts in Japanese Society and Business to Slow Down* (Japan for Sustainability)

> *'In Japan, the concept of a 'lifestyle of health and sustainability' (LOHAS) has been gaining popularity, along with a 'slow life' movement that has been booming for several years. These movements are evident in books, magazine feature articles, websites, and newspapers ads. Some big bookstores have a section dedicated to slow life and slow food. You can even hear 'slow music' on Japanese airlines. What kind of potential do these movements have in Japanese society? The desire for slower lifestyles might work as a leverage point to depart from our present growth-oriented society. Not only individuals but also companies are now making efforts for this kind of social change. Perhaps the country is entering into an exciting era.'*

(LOHAS; Green Business)

We yearn for simpler life with more meaning. If only we could have the best of both worlds.

In Totnes, Devon, I met artist Jeanine de Waele, whose beautiful pictures express her message.

*'Poppy Fields' by Jeanine de Waele*

31

*When I observe nature through painting for hours immersed in the natural world, I become aware of the inherent perfection and grandeur of Nature. The timing of emerging buds, the opening of certain flowers with the change of quality of light. It is perfect and we are part of that perfection even though we forget it by becoming victims of our minds.*

*I can see that when I am immersed in life, I lose touch with that perfection because of being in another mindset, one in which my thoughts and feelings can sometimes dictate to me e.g fear of lack, greed, lust etc. This is how I lose touch with this inherent perfection that is there even though we have lost touch.*

*I am not a victim to my mind and the memory of perfection is always there.*

*Art has always been a powerful means to get into my right mind and transcend the ego tendencies'.*

Jeanine de Waele, painter, Totnes, Devon

Dennis Potter, knowing the end of his life was approaching, expressed similar awareness of the beauty of the natural world. Better not to wait until then:

*'The now-ness of everything is absolutely wonderful.'*

Dennis Potter

*Jamaican fishermen*

## Chapter 2
# But There is a Downside –
# We Face a Global Crisis

## The environmental crisis and global economic and social injustice

*'The global war on terror is diverting the world's attention from the central causes of instability. Acts of terror and the dangerous reactions they provoke are symptomatic of underlying sources of global insecurity, including the perilous interplay among poverty, infectious disease, environmental degradation, and rising competition over oil and other resources.'*

World Watch Institute, Annual State of the World 2005

*'What if we discover our present way of life is irreconcilable with our vocation to become fully human?'*

Paulo Freire

**We face a frightening crisis – if only we allow ourselves to feel it.** I sometimes wonder if we are becoming numb as a way of coping with the horrors we see daily on our TV screens, the fear and insecurity of life in the 21st Century, which is paradoxically the most plentiful yet. Numbness blocks feelings that would change the world.

It is not unlike life many centuries ago except: *so much more is possible – both bad but especially GOOD.* Yet, despite all our resources and skills, our world is far from being the world of our dreams that it could be. It really is a crazy world.

**Sustainability in the broadest sense – environmental, social and economic – is the most urgent issue facing people everywhere.** Sustainability is being redefined to include far more than the environment and concern for the planet. It embraces all those activities that lead to an *unsustainable* global society. Of course, the two aspects are closely linked.

I asked Sally Oakes at the Centre for Alternative Technology, Machynlleth in Wales, for a definition of sustainability. She said:

*'Meeting the needs of the present without compromising the ability of future generations to meet their own needs is still good if fairly simplistic. Sustainability must include both social and economic factors as well as the environment, if we are to deal with the causes of the problems. We have chosen the three key areas of climate change, biodiversity and habitat, and social and international equity as our key sustainability challenges. These have been prioritised because they could become irreversible, or out of control.'*

---

### The Big Issues

- **Environmental and ecological degradation and climate change**
- **Growing poverty gap** - between rich and powerful elites and poor nations and the poor
- **Enormous, growing indebtedness and interest repayments**
- **Underlying lack of respect for difference and human dignity** - how to make diversity a source of delight, wealth and creativity rather than discrimination, exploitation and violent conflict
- **Lack of opportunity for the majority** - people and families need security, stability, education and health
- **The gap between top people who make strategic decisions and people on the ground** - those most affected and who have practical understanding of the situation
- **Reluctance to share power**, or speak the truth, in a spirit of universal mutual respect and partnership
- **Greed and corruption** - little difference; disproportionate rewards for the few *
- **The underlying value**, corporate duty, is making money rather than meeting human needs
- **Global sourcing and agribusiness** - mixed blessings

---

- **Unfair trade**; unrepresentative Global Institutions (WTO and IMF); imposing on other cultures
- **The power and instability of financial markets**
- **Trans-national Corporations** (TNCs) - bigger economies, more powerful than nations - undermining Democracy
- **Business externalises** or exports the social costs it creates
- **Public services, increasingly, can't cope**
- **Widespread de-skilling** - loss of in depth professional, technical and trades experience, traditional knowledge and skills - making things, growing food, understanding of cultivation in adverse climates and soils
- **Avoidable death and disease** (poverty 50,000 deaths per day), pollution, unhealthy eating and lifestyles, tobacco, alcohol, road deaths and injuries (3,000 deaths per day), civil war, genocide, war, 'natural' disasters and international 'terrorism'
- **Loss of confidence in leaders and current democracy**
- **A quest for meaning, values, spirit and balance**

(* *UK FTSE: 100 companies average CEO £2.1m; national average salary £22,411. 350 companies directors up 8.4% compared with 3.35% shop floor in 2005; City bonuses £7.5bn; 3000 city workers given at least £1m; meanwhile: house repossessions, highest since 1991; mortgage arrears up 21% ; 70,000 will go bankrupt (Boom and Bust Britain, Independent, 5-1-06)*

**This US, Anglo-Saxon, form of Globalisation is unsustainable** – creating environmental degradation and climate change on a massive and ever-increasing scale that threatens our existence. It is destroying ecological diversity, communities and patterns of life, especially those of the poor, the agricultural work of women and centuries of ancient knowledge of agriculture.

**There is a growing poverty gap.** It's *'trickle up'* not *'trickle down'*. Basically, globalisation works for a rich, powerful elite. The roots of unsustainability are huge disparities in wealth and power and the growing gap between rich and poor. The West is exporting Victorian dirty jobs. To a degree, it is a new form of empire and slavery. Getting products made more cheaply in developing countries is a mixed benefit. It helps development but comes at an environmental cost – not only the cost of transportation but also increased pollution because environmental standards are currently mostly lower than in USA or Europe.

**For the mass of human beings, globalisation is not working** – not at least in its present form. For those relative few of us, the 'in-betweens', it works to a degree but at a huge cost, personal and environmental. We are 'enslaved' by it and heading for what looks like disaster.

**Globalisation works best** (though perhaps not at a spiritual level) **for a tiny elite of very rich and powerful people** but not for the mass of six billion human beings throughout the world, 85% of whom live on $5.98 per day (World Bank) and one billion on less than a dollar. In contrast, Bill Gates receives £60m in annual Microsoft dividends. Meanwhile 225 people own more wealth than the poorest 2.5 billion (*UNDP Human Development Report*, 1998). The Walton family, richest in the world, who own Wal-Mart, the world's largest retailer, is worth about $98 billion whilst their army of employees are reputed to be amongst the worst paid employees in USA, their low wages supplemented by government food vouchers. Recently, Wal-Mart has been ordered to pay $172m (£99m) in compensation to workers who were refused lunch breaks. They face mounting claims and bad publicity.

**Of course, the terminology is wrong.** Globalisation has existed for centuries and though often brutal, on balance it has brought rich benefits to humanity. It is the current global economic system that is not working – the doctrine of free market capitalism, consumerism, continuous economic growth, the unproven 'trickle down' theory and imposition of free market doctrines of universal privatisation and industrialisation of agriculture. The ordinary people of Russia have suffered badly from suddenly importing raw capitalism. Over two hundred years ago, Adam Smith, supposed author of the free market doctrine, warned of the dangers of unfettered free trade.

**Maybe what we call globalisation is really 'US Americanisation' or 'Anglo Saxon Westernisation' and colonisation.** Consumerism, and the pursuit of economic growth and power are leading to spiritual poverty. We export a silly, disempowering celebrity culture promoting false values. A widespread backlash is emerging, especially from people in Europe and the Muslim world. Alternatives will emerge. A living system works this way. The rapid development of China and India adds to the urgency of finding better models.

**The *re-emergence* of the ancient civilisations** of China, India, Islam, Latin America and Africa offers the opportunity for benign change in the longer term, especially if we all adopt the role of partners.

———————oooooooOooooooo———————

# The environmental emergency

The world's greatest environmental challenge is:

*'So far-reaching in its impact and irreversible in its destructive power, that it alters radically human existence.'*
Tony Blair, preparing for Presidency of G8 and the EU

**The environmental crisis endangers life on the planet.** We face an escalating emergency. There is growing recognition that climate change is the greatest threat we face, far greater than terrorism, which can just divert our attention. We have no idea how close we are to upsetting the current equilibrium. We risk massive, unpredictable and irreversible ecological change. Clearly the process is already advanced. In 2005, we had the hottest ever October and the most severe hurricanes on record.

**The current scientific consensus is that greenhouse gas emissions need to be cut by 60% by mid-century.** Yet even if the Kyoto Protocol were implemented, emissions would rise 30% in a decade. Meanwhile seas are rising; there is an increasing risk of flooding our homes, and cities such as London; some species of fish are moving North; other species are disappearing; our soil in Europe is becoming degraded and our climate gets more unstable and hotter. Current research indicates that the 'climate conveyor belt' that keeps Western Europe warm, may be changing as a result of melting ice in the Arctic. If this is confirmed, we might ultimately face a much colder climate! Coasts and marine life around Britain are under pressure from pollution from fertilisers and pesticides, coastal erosion, over-fishing and climate change. The poor in Africa are likely to suffer most of all, as drought worsens and they lose their cattle and crops. Nations in the South wait for the rich countries to put their house in order.

**It is not just climate change; it is the incapacity of the Earth to meet the rapidly growing needs of humanity**. I was shocked as I read the startling information in Herbert Girardet's *Cities People Planet* (Girardet, H, 2004). Here are some of the data.

## The Human Consumption Crisis

- Already humanity substantially exceeds the planet's capacity to meet its consumption of renewable resources
- Rapid development in Asia - China, India and SE
- As countries develop, they expect US/EU lifestyle
- The worldwide move from rural to city living: 47% 2000; 60% 2060
- Mega cities (i.e. over 10m) growth: 1950 = one; 2000 = 19; 2015 = 23, 15 in Asia
- China expects to build 400 new cities by 2010
- Cars in China: 15.5m 2002; 156m by 2020, i.e. 20m per year
- London's footprint is 293 times its area = 2 x productive land of UK; rich cities can be anything to 500 x their surface area
- If everyone lived as we do in London, 3 planets would be needed to support us; LA = 5 planets

**A huge and foolish distraction.** After digesting this, I thought: In comparison with the environmental crisis and poverty, the 'war on terror', i.e. on Iraq, seems like a huge and foolish distraction from the biggest threats to humanity, wasting lives and billions of dollars and pounds, far better spent on addressing the real crisis. We face an emergency and we are ignoring it.

**The news each day is frightening.** Yet most of us act as if unaware of the need for urgent and far-reaching action. Numb perhaps, like animals frozen in headlights, we continue our business and lifestyles as if there is 'no problem'.

**We need a new economic model** to replace the current fossil fuel, automobile-centred, throw-away, mass consumer society pioneered by USA in the 1940s, with help from Freud's daughter, Anna, in installing it into the public's unconscious. We need political leaders who no longer think only in terms of continuous economic growth, Gross Domestic Product as the measure of progress and rushing in to grab a share of the opportunities in the rest of the world. Current US and European ways of life, replicated throughout the world, are completely unsustainable. USA, with only 4% of the world's population, uses 42% of its gasoline and creates 25% of its pollution. Greenhouse gas is predicted to rise by 52% by 2030 unless the world takes urgent action to reduce energy consumption (*World Energy Outlook* report from the International Energy Agency). Meanwhile, 45 million new cars are produced every year! The USA, the richest and most powerful nation blocks attempts like Kyoto, to reach global agreements.

**China will soon overtake the USA as the world's largest emitter of $CO_2$.** The extraordinary growth of the Chinese and Indian economies is changing everything. It is Britain of the nineteenth century all over again. The Chinese economy is growing at 16.5 % per annum (not the official figure) consuming huge and rapidly increasing quantities of the world's resources. Already, China is no longer self-sufficient in food. The world's second-largest energy consumer uses more of the earth's resources than the USA and will overtake them as top emitter of greenhouse gases by 2025. That will dwarf any cuts in $CO_2$ the rest of the world can make. Cars are rapidly replacing bicycles, now banned in some big cities. Large numbers of new coalmines are being opened. Five of the world's ten most polluted cities, including Beijing, where there are no more smog free days, are in China.

# A dangerous future

*'Soaring fuel prices, rumours of winter power cuts, panic over the gas supply from Russia, abrupt changes to forecasts of crude output ... it's time to face the fact that the supplies we so depend on are going to run out.'*

Independent Extra, 20-1-2006 and Leggett, J, 2006.

Recently Russia cut off supplies and then we heard rumours of Russia buying the UK gas company, Centrica. The combination of dependency on oil and gas, water shortage and instability in the Middle East usher in the spectre of a Third World War over resources leaving us feeling more vulnerable and stressed.

There are wiser solutions than aggressive global politics, **not including nuclear power** with its continuing, enormous and unpredictable costs, unanswered disposal problem, and horrifying scenario of a nuclear terrorist threat. When people advocate the use of nuclear for clean energy, they conveniently forget to include the environmental costs of mining uranium, transporting it and processing it.

> 'We would live with much increased risk of losing whole cities
> to suitcase bombers.'          Jeremy Leggett

Billions of pounds would be needed in perpetuity. New stations would not come on stream in the UK much before 2020. Britain has 2.3 cubic metres of dangerous nuclear waste, estimated to cost £85bn to bury. A tiny amount would kill an adult in 2 minutes (Leggett, J, 2006). They also forget that uranium is not a renewable resource and hence neither is it nuclear power (*Ecology Magazine*). Developing nuclear power is not a sensible example for mature, developed countries to set – whilst, ironically, opposing Iran's right to do the same.

**It is the difference between yin and yang**. It is important to see the situation with awareness and wisdom, not driven by anachronistic impulses, panic or distressed desire to leave a legacy. Today, it not sensible always to solve problems with big money, big business, big science, big simple solutions, making big money, colonising and wielding big power. Is it also worth mentioning that huge wind turbines need concrete foundations that release as much $CO_2$ in their construction as will be saved by generating power through wind. Large-scale centralised solutions and dependence on resources supplied from other countries, leave us vulnerable in several senses – from supply, toxicity and attack. **We need to learn from nature**, which uses a wide range of diverse solutions, many of which are local.

**The wise way: develop a multitude of low-carbon renewable alternative energy sources** such as hydrogen, solar, wind and water power, bio-fuels, cleaner auto engines, cleaning up current power stations, localised energy provision, home energy provision, saving waste of energy, offering new non-polluting or less polluting energy sources to developing countries – the cheapest, preferably local, ones to poorer countries. We already have the solutions we need and the cost will be far less, leaving money for more important needs such as health, education and poverty reduction.

We can learn from good  models.

## Good Models

**Sweden**, a country of 9 million people plans to become the world's first practically oil-free economy. A committee of industrialists, academics, farmers, car makers, civil servants and others, will report to parliament in several months, trying to wean the country off oil completely within 15 years - without building a new generation of nuclear power stations. There will be a 15-year limit set for switching to renewable energy. Biofuels will be included, preferred to further nuclear power (John Vidal, *Guardian* environment editor 8-2- 2006)

**Germany, Japan, China, Cuba** and **India** provide good models for the world. Germany has led the way in Europe in almost every respect: research, far-sighted development of waste disposal, energy saving and alternatives sources of heat and power. I believe they pursue wise foreign policies.

**Japan's** energy use has remained unchanged since 1973 while output has tripled. Japan's government has subsidised $1.3bn worth of residential solar systems and provided a tax break for fuel-efficient cars including hybrids. (*Ecologist* July/August 2005).

**Japan** is also the second largest aid donor in the world. Over the past 30 years, it has provided over $200 billion to development as part of its ethical and astute assistance programme. Top recipients of Japan's aid are countries in East and South East Asia. Also it is one of the largest donors in several African countries. This is wise strategy. In the past five years, Japan's Overseas Development Aid has increased from $8.8 billion in 2000 to $13.5 billion in 2004. At the G8 Gleneagles Summit, Prime Minister Koizumi pledged to increase aid by $10 billion in the coming five years. Japan has also agreed on a debt-cancellation package to Africa and promised to contribute approximately $4.9 billion, one of the largest pledges among donor nations. (Norway, Luxembourg, Denmark, Sweden, Neth-erlands, Portugal give the highest aid as a percent of GDP - OECD).

**China's** 5-year development plan aims for a 20% increase in energy efficiency. China has launched an $80 million programme with the United Nations to promote efficient use of energy and cut pollution. It aims to quadruple GDP by 2020 while just doubling its energy consumption. Her programme aims to reduce energy consumption by nearly 19 million tonnes of coal equivalent in the first three-year phase of the programme, cutting carbon emissions by 12 million tonnes. China is likely to be the leading country for renewable energy. China is creating the world's first sustainable cities, starting with Dongtan.

**Cuba** rid itself of a corrupt, US supported regime in 1959. The withdrawal of ex-USSR oil and chemical fertilisers and the hypocritical US embargo forced her to become organic and almost self-sufficient – at a cost to aircraft safety and opportunities for its talented people. Havana is a model for urban agriculture and 'sustainable city,' local organic food growing on every bit of spare ground. Much of the food eaten by citizens is grown by communities, hospitals, old people's homes and schools in beautiful *organoponicos*, enriched with compost from city waste, the surplus sold in community markets. Cuba has excellent health, research and education, achieving the highest world standards at low cost; has bottom-up democracy; and supports poor countries. (HDRA, Cuba Organic Support Group; *Havana Journal*; Fidel Castro's excellent principled book, *'Tomorrow is too late,'* on sustainability from a different viewpoint).

**India** is developing a wealth of initiatives in local, alternative, renewable energy technologies for rural areas (BBC World Service and Google).

**Spain** has installed wind power, second only to Germany, and above USA. The number of turbines exceeds 10,000, now in sight all over in Spain. Constructing large wind turbines does create as much pollution as is saved however.

**Australia**, where sun is abundant, is experimenting with solar power. *'Technically you could supply all of the world's energy needs by covering 4% of the world's desert area with photo-voltaic panels,'* says Martin Green from the Advanced Silicon Photo-voltaics and Photonics research centre at the University of New South Wales in Sydney. It is expensive but that will change – probably cheaper at the end of the day, and certainly cheaper than violence, war, disease and poverty. Lynn and Chris Stevenson, in Robertson, New South Wales, meet their needs with wind and solar power. *'All our power is run by solar and wind energy and we're learning how to manage that and how it works in our house.'*

**Africa, Cuba** and **USA** have abundant sunshine. Solar Electric Light Fund, a non-profit charitable organisation promotes, develops and facilitates solar rural electrification and energy self-sufficiency in developing countries. Amongst their partnerships are Brightening Lives with Solar Schools and Energy, in Kwa Zulu-Natal South Africa and a rural solar project in Nigeria (SELF). Cuba uses the solar energy for cooking.

*Cooking with solar energy in Cuba*

——————————ooooooooOoooooo——————————

# The crisis caused by global social injustice and violence

Not fully recognised, is the crisis caused by global social injustice and violent, cynical foreign policies that don't work.

*'The world will not be peaceful or safe unless we attend*
*to the poorest places.'*
Clare Short, former Minister for Overseas Development

The horrors in Iraq, Sudan and Palestine are three of many examples. Hostility to the 'West' in Islamic countries, within our own alienated communities too, is a major threat to security, peace of mind as well as the interests of all humanity. Iraq is an example of 'heavy blundering in.'

**'War against terror' does not work** because there can be no peace without justice. Intelligence comes from people whose hearts and minds are supportive. People, especially the young and disillusioned, who feel unheard, become radicalised. They are easy prey to being recruited as suicide bombers when they lose hope of participating in the creation of a fair society. Being a young person in any society can be difficult, a time of angst and uncertainty. Suicide is highest amongst young men. Exclusion and desperation lead to violence. Violent responses breed more violence. Violence does not address underlying issues. Justice is not being delivered in Palestine or to many other Muslim peoples. Malcolm X was right to say people do 'whatever is necessary'.

*'Only justice, not bombs, can make our dangerous world a safer place'.*
Robert Fisk

In December 2005, a wave of fire and violence in France expressed the anger of alienated and frustrated youths from immigrant families.

Part of the mess results from a long history of cynical foreign policies primarily based on pursuing 'Western' economic and political interests, by whatever means – mirrors again – including regime change, creating countries, supporting corrupt tyrannies and overthrowing left wing democracies, e.g. in Latin America. Double standards and hypocrisy are obvious to ordinary people if not to their perpetrators.

---

## The Dark Side

**One third of deaths - some 18 million people a year or 50,000 per day - are due to poverty-related causes.** That's 270 million people since 1990, the majority women and children, roughly equal to the population of the US (Millennium Campaign). Every day, 25,000 to 30,000 people die because they do not have enough food or water. 6 million children under five die needlessly every year (*Lancet*, June 2003).

**Most of the thousands of deaths in so-called 'natural disasters'** affect or are associated with poor people and are caused by not respecting the living system or old knowledge of the dangers. Drug crop growing is associated with poverty too - most people prefer to earn a living ethically if they can.

**Not 'trickle down' but 'trickle up.'** Between the 1930s and the 1980s, the gap between rich and poor in the UK was closing. But, for the last 20 years, for many in rich countries and most people in the poorest, things have got worse. In the US, many people are worse off or at least very little better off, while the rich are vastly richer. The official U.N. statistics show that over 12 percent of the United States population - or about 37 million people - lived in poverty in 2004, with nearly 16 percent - or about 46 million - without health insurance. In USA more than 38 million people, including 14 million children, are threatened by lack of food. (National Economic and Social Rights Initiative). 12% of people in USA live below the official poverty line. In Washington DC, seat of

---

government, the figure is 19.9%. Growing numbers are without health insurance.

*'As the wealthiest country on Earth, with higher per capita income levels than any other country, the United States has ... one of the highest incidences of poverty among the rich industrialised nations.'*
Dr. Arjun Sengupta, United Nations rights expert (worldnet)

**Venezuela may be an exception.** To the consternation of the US political establishment, Venezuela's left wing president, Hugo Chavez, is trying to use oil wealth to help the poor and set a *'trickle down'* trend in Latin America. (Johann Hari, *Independent,* 19-8-2005)

**The cost of so-called 'value for money' resulting from global sourcing and cost cutting is not included in the lower prices we pay at the till.** While a few super rich grow richer, more people in the world are reduced to extreme poverty. Working people here suffer insecurity, their pay and benefits decline and pension plans are cut as their work is outsourced, their jobs migrate or are eliminated. It is an outrage we need to allow ourselves to feel.

**The number of hungry people in developing countries increased** by 18% in the second half of the 1990s to some 800 million today. Worldwide, nearly 2 billion people suffer from hunger and chronic nutrient deficiencies (Worldwatch). In sub-Saharan Africa, average life expectancy is now 47 years. It would have been 62 years had it not been for the AIDS and HIV epidemic, partly due to the lack of drugs available in the West. AIDS is having a devastating effect on African economies. Since the late 1970s, more than 23 million people have lost their lives to the disease. By 2010, the cumulative toll is expected to rise to 45 million (UNICEF)

In **India**, while benefiting some, rapid development has not benefited India's 550 million farmers many of whom suffer dire poverty and are deep in debt. Many commit suicide, often using the chemicals that got them into debt. 500 million people in India are below the poverty line. In **Bhopal**, some 3,000 people died and more than half a million people were seriously injured on December 3, 1984 when lethal gas was released from Union Carbide's facility. Another 10,000 to 50,000 more deaths are linked to the disaster. Only part of the compensation, worth less than $500m, has reached the victims.

**Millions of men, women and children around the world are forced to lead lives as slaves.** Slavery is illegal in every country but there are more slaves than ever – an estimated 27 million. Four million women and children are trafficked every year, one million for prostitution. Although this exploitation is often not called slavery, the conditions are the same. People are sold like objects, forced to work for little or no pay and are at the mercy of their 'employers'. (Anti-Slavery International)

**Industrialising agriculture.** The World Development Movement says,

*'Agriculture is first and foremost about allowing people to live.'*

The **'Green Revolution'**, a phrase first coined in 1968, appeared to offer great benefits in the form of cheaper food and less arduous work. However proponents of industrialising agriculture and crops for export did not anticipate the destructive effects on the mass of human beings; the capacity of the poor to feed themselves; the natural environment; the complex ecology of the soil with all its hidden insects; the effect that it would have on nutrition – our main source of health – plant life, other creatures, water and weather systems; small farmers producing local food; communities; rural women in India and Africa; and the ensuing loss of ancient knowledge of cultivation. Industrialising agriculture, crops and animal production for cheap meat and milk, reduces the quality of our food and our health and results in more and more pandemics (World Watch).

**Patenting outrage:** Patenting by trans-national corporations (TNCs), of plants and seeds traditionally saved by farmers from year to year and ancient pest control using extracts from plants and trees is greedy exploitation. TNCs have steadily bought up seed companies in India and elsewhere.

**Creeping homogeneity** handicaps the ability of farmers everywhere to respond to pests, disease and changes in climate – and has ruined many of our towns. EU registration of vegetable seeds that are for sale has led to a huge loss of varieties except in seed libraries such as the one provided by the Henry Doubleday Research Association (HDRA). Organic farmers in England are being priced out of farming, forced out by big business buying up the land, against which they cannot compete. Since the beginning of the last century, 75 percent of genetic diversity of food crops has been lost. Scientific innovation can benefit mankind if it works with nature. The ugliness occurs when it is based, however 'unawarely,' on greed for profit and domination, 'colonising' in the broadest sense, obsession with technology.

*'Technological civilisation is destroying nature and human life.'*
Jerry Mander

**Genetic Modification (GM),** a violence against nature, is temporarily in retreat in the UK and Europe because of public protest and consumer choice. The corporate argument is blatantly dishonest - largely on the basis of 'scientific evidence' that GM products have not proved harmful to humans.

The equally important issues of the effect on ecological diversity, the unpredictability of the consequences of tinkering with nature and the contamination of GM free and organic crops are not addressed. The World Trade Organisation (WTO) has just ruled that the European Union illegally stopped imports of genetically modified organisms from the US. A final ruling will not be made until the year-end. Unfortunately, more than 30 GMOs or derived food and animal feed products have been approved for marketing in the EU. However, countries such as Austria, France, Germany, Greece and Luxembourg still have national bans on some types of GM maize and rapeseed.

**People need to be ready to campaign again, responsibly, in whatever way is necessary.**

**The Eight UN Millennium Development Goals** were agreed in September 2000. The eight Millennium Development Goals – which range from halving extreme poverty to halting the spread of HIV/AIDS and providing universal primary education, all by the target date of 2015 – formed a blueprint agreed to by all the world's countries and all the world's leading development institutions.

*'We will have time to reach the Millennium Development Goals – worldwide and in most, or even all, individual countries – but only if we break with business as usual. We cannot win overnight. Success will require sustained action across the entire decade between now and the deadline. It takes time to train the teachers, nurses and engineers; to build the roads, schools and hospitals; to grow the small and large businesses able to create the jobs and income needed. So we must start now. And we must more than double global development assistance over the next few years. Nothing less will help to achieve the Goals.'*
Kofi Annan, United Nations Secretary-General

Measured against this challenge, progress is slow.

*African village*

The Royal Africa Society says:

*'It's not just about thinking up good things we should do to Africa – it's about the bad things we should stop doing.'*
Richard Dowden, Director, Royal Africa Society

**Rhetoric or substance?** Tony Blair was inspired when he called Africa *'a scar on the conscience of the world.'* Is Britain helping to heal it or are we doing the reverse?

His statement about debt forgiveness and aid came from the right place. Britain is not implementing the UN Convention on Corruption and curbing the activities of British arms dealers, both actions urged by Tony Blair's Commission for Africa (Amnesty International and Royal Africa Society).

*'Signing cheques for debt relief or aid is one thing. Changing laws and systems is more difficult but if the British government is serious about helping Africa, that is what it must do.'*
Richard Dowden

Doing right takes courage.
**Real solutions to Africa's problems are likely to come from**

**Africans,** says the World Development Movement. Tony Blair means well, but can't see that his current approach is *'insulting, lacks transparency and involves condescending colonial attitudes.'* **Charity, though desperately needed – and it makes us feel better – does not address the underlying causes. That requires a fundamental shift in the 'West' including getting used to less.**

The 'West' needs to support Africa and African institutions in finding their own solutions, not ours.

*African houses – under construction and complete*

————————————ooooooo**O**ooooooo————————

**We are part of a living system.** Human society is part of an interconnected living ecosystem. Human beings are members of a global community. What happens in other parts of the world, especially in other cultures and the less economically developed world, affects everyone. ***To enjoy a sustainable future, everyone needs to be a world citizen.*** We are all responsible. Perhaps born again Christian, George Bush and his Neo-Conservative colleagues and the phenomenon of Osama Bin Laden, Al-Qaida and Fundamentalism mirror reflections of each other. US refusal to allow UN unimpeded interviews with prisoners in Guantanamo Bay is a mirror image of Syria's similar refusal to allow UN unimpeded access in their inquiry into the murder of former Lebanese PM Rafik Hariri in Lebanon (Amnesty International). We are driving the Middle East into the arms of other countries and 'extremists.' Read Robert Fisk in UK's *Independent* newspaper.

## The key things to remember are:

*'Any living system that is not respected, hits back harshly.'*

*'When people do not learn willingly, the Universe forces it on them.'*

This Karma principle applies both to our environment and the global society in which social and economic justice is needed.

*'Colonisation is over.'*

Another:                *'Truth will always out.'*

**If we don't learn from history, hostility to the 'West' will grow.** The dire consequences we face have their roots in a history of exploitation, interference and lack of respect in the Middle East from the Crusades onward, but especially since the end of World War 1. We are in denial.

*The Welsh Assembly Building*

## Chapter 3
# Business is a Major Force for Good

**Seeing opportunities in the big issues is the key to long-term success.** Sustainability requires us to see the big issues as opportunities to be grasped – not denied or avoided. Businesses thrive in the long term by continuously responding to big issues, creatively and positively. New products and enterprises begin this way.

**Business is good at making some things happen efficiently.** Business, often in partnership with government and universities, is a force for innovation and transformation. Think of the transformations brought about by Thomas Newcomen's first successful steam engine in 1712, later developed by James Watt and Richard Trevithick, Henry Ford's Model T, Marconi's wireless, Sir Alexander Fleming's discovery of penicillin, Boeing, facilitating mass air travel, Sir Tim Berners-Lee's invention of the internet, Bill Gates' Microsoft operating system, Steve Jobs' Apple, both entrepreneurs who helped take the PC and internet to its massive use today – all seeing opportunities in big issues. In the mid-19th Century, Edward Johns saw the opportunity to prevent cholera and typhoid epidemics in cities and started manufacturing 'johns', as some still call the WC.

**The Big Issues, today are global, social, ethical and ecological.** The best way forward for business is to see all Big Issues listed in Chapter 2 figure 1, as opportunities for *good business* – often in partnership with NGOs, charities, national, state or local government.

---

### A Big Issue Opportunity

**'Western Empire' is in <u>relative</u> decline.** The new global, economic powers are China, India, Brazil, others in SE Asia, and Latin America perhaps followed by the Middle East. We have to face reality, give up old colonial domination, and embrace the new. We risk making enemies of countries where there is oil and gas. Iranian President, Mahmoud Ahmadinejad, is telling the 'West' to stop bullying and accept that it needs Iran more than Iran needs it. Developing and sharing sustainable technologies, sources of power and cities may be a part of a better way of working with the perceived threat he poses.

It means having long vision and grasping new opportunities offered by Big Issues, changing our role completely - humbly joining the rest of the world as partners in something mature and appropriate - giving up old habits of colonisation.

---

**Positive news.** Every day, there is exciting, positive news. Companies, many of them small new enterprises, and entrepreneurs, sometimes in partnership with universities and government take initiatives to improve the situation, find solutions and move things forward. We only hear a fraction of it! A benign process is going on. Human creativity is endless. Unfortunately bad news sells papers. But dwelling on it depresses us and diverts our energy from being creative in changing things for the better. UK's monthly *'Positive News'* is a source of worldwide positive news.

**We need to be challenged as well.** Fundamental systemic change is urgently needed. As argued elsewhere, to make transformation easier, government and international institutions must create a level playing field and set long-term strategy that business can respond to.

**Change comes about in all sorts of little ways.** All kinds of good business contributions are reported every day. There is an abundance of good news in Ethical Corporation, Ethical Performance and Business in the Community websites. These are to be valued as steady improvement in ethical, sustainable practice and contributions to the local community. My cynic says: 'not radical enough' and 'palliative charity.' Most are incremental; some more about reputation, basically 'green washing'; some are the best companies think they can do within the existing system. Companies with doubtful records, to say the least, still in essentially damaging businesses they need to get out of, are forming partnerships with well-known NGOs – constructive engagement which is to be welcomed.

**Preparing us for change.** Whatever it is, whatever the motivations, it all makes a difference, raising awareness and equipping us to make more fundamental changes.

---

## Good Business

**Interface** is something fundamental - a rare, outstanding example of business at its best. Interface's principle is 'do well by doing good,' says septuagenarian, Ray Anderson, Chairman and founder of Interface. Companies like this are a minority but their number is growing, often from small beginnings. Sustainability is at the heart of Interface, a worldwide company producing floor coverings, fabrics for airliner seats, speciality chemicals and interior architectural products. Interface aims for a 'zero footprint' and is more than half way there (Interface). It creates a host of sustainable companies in its supply chain. Ray recently donated to the Friends Meeting House on Euston Road, London, a recyclable carpet made from cornstarch for their main conference room.

**Arup and the sustainable city.** Arup work as a strategic partner with Shanghai Industrial Investment Corporation on the World's first sustainable city, Dongtan. Arup has signed a multi-billion contract to build a string of 'eco-cities' - large, self- sustaining urban centres around China of which this is the first. These are intended to be self-sufficient in energy, water, and most food products and with zero emissions of greenhouse gases in their transport systems. They will provide important models for the world.

**The Welsh Assembly Building is a beacon.** Costing £67m, officially opened 1st March, St David's Day, it was created by the Richard Rogers Partnership, BDSP Partnership and Arup and Taylor Woodrow Construction. The design brief required it to achieve an 'Excellent' certification under the Building Research Establishment Environmental Assessment Method (BREEAM). It meets these targets and the Assembly's constitutional responsibilities for sustainable development: design life of 100 years; indigenous materials; minimum energy consumption and waste; renewable technologies; an 'exemplar' in terms of sustainability; an environmental design. It uses natural ventilation and passive systems to heat and cool the building, reducing running costs for the building by 30-50%. The central cooling system is

---

an Earth Heat Exchange System providing the highest efficiency possible. Heating for the building is a wood fired boiler system also providing the highest efficiency possible. Wood as a fuel source is effectively carbon neutral; gives low $CO_2$ emissions and uses wood chips or wood pellets provided locally. Approximately 50% Welsh labour and materials were used equating to £15m of the construction cost.

**Sherwood Energy Village,** Ollerton, Nottinghamshire is another model business initiative, created by ex-miners including executive director Stan Crawford. SEV is a mixed-use, environmentally friendly development on the site of a former coalmine, which closed in 1994 with the loss of 600 jobs. Over 500 jobs in various industries have been created. Mr Crawford expects that number to rise to over 1,500 by 2008 as new businesses open. An industrial wasteland has been transformed into green parkland and environmentally friendly buildings. It involved excavating and recycling over 100,000 tons of concrete. 196 eco-friendly homes, designed to attract families and workers will be constructed. Buildings will use turbines and pumps, rather than gas, to heat them. Ollerton is an example of a prospering community that has recovered from the loss of its traditional source of employment. Mr Crawford and colleagues aimed *'to do three things: create jobs, diversify the economic base, and do it without the muck that mining produces.'* Also *'It was about having a say; it was about democracy.'* Last year SEV was named winner of the DTI's first Enterprising Britain award. Enterprising Britain 2006 is a national competition to find the place that best exemplifies the enterprise spirit. (*Independent on Sunday* 12-3-06)

**Small businesses provide models too.** Charlotte Vøhtz started her organic toiletries company, **Green People**, in 1997, from her kitchen table, sourcing natural and organic raw materials. It took off and she needed a new office and a warehouse. This gave the opportunity to build her environmental principles into the very fabric of the new premises. Her offices are designed without air conditioning. Instead the building has passive cooling. An atrium down the middle of the offices and windows opening in the roof provide a vent so that cool air is drawn up from the basement. Staff travel to business meetings only if the likely outcome is to grow the renewable energy market; then the train is given preference. **Good Energy** is introducing a measure for $CO_2$ emissions per staff member and will award bonuses based on reducing their carbon emissions in work travel.

BedZed Beddington Zero Energy Development, in Sutton, is a beacon, showing how the demand for eco-friendly, affordable and attractive housing offering an easy lifestyle can be met without destroying the countryside. The mix of housing and workspace combines up-to-date thinking on sustainable development in energy-efficient design and only uses renewable energy for heating from sources on site. It is the first large-scale 'carbon neutral' community, i.e. it adds no carbon dioxide to the atmosphere (BedZed).

**Bill Gates has pledged $900m to fight against TB.** This is benign. There is a tradition of corporate giving in USA. I reflected on Getty, Rhodes and others in the 19C who made vast fortunes in ruthless and sometimes violent ways and later created foundations. *Should such vast sums be in the hands of individuals, to dispose of, in the first place? Do they do it better?* If we bring about systemic change, there will be much less need for 'charity.' However, Charitable Trusts established by 19th Century entrepreneurs like Joseph Rowntree enable revolutionary research today.

## Partnerships are making fundamental contributions

**Catholic Agency for Overseas Development (CAFOD)** through rigorous research and astute campaigning, is highly effective in helping global corporations like IBM, HP and Dell, to rapidly establish and implement their own industry codes of conduct for workers' conditions in companies in poorer countries, manufacturing parts or assembling products (CAFOD).

**New Apollo Project** is another example of 'do well by doing good.' This US alliance of labour, environmental, civil rights, business and political leaders has laid out a vision to create new jobs and achieve energy independence in ten years. It aims to unify the country behind a 10-year programme of strategic investment for clean energy technology and new infrastructure. It has received support from 17 of America's largest labour unions as well as a broad cross-section of the environmental movement, including the Sierra Club, the Natural Resources Defence Council (NRDC), the Union of Concerned Scientists and Greenpeace. Perryman (2004), advising on the Apollo Alliance project:

*'If economists agree on anything, it's that inventing new technologies and creating whole new industries is what America does best. We are a creative economy, not a commodity economy. This project would keep us on the cutting edge of manufacturing emerging technologies and secure our long-term prosperity.'*

Proposed tax credits and investments would **create 3.3 million new, high-wage jobs** for manufacturing, construction, transportation, high-tech and public sector workers, whilst reducing dependence on imported oil and cleaning the air. It would also position USA to take the lead in fast-growing markets, dramatically reduce trade deficit as well as more than pay for itself in energy savings and returns to the US Treasury. Oilman Bush is just showing signs of seeing the light!

**'Out of the box' Woking Borough Council – a microcosm of what can be done.** Woking Borough Council has cut carbon-dioxide emissions by 77 per cent since 1990 using a hybrid-energy system involving small private electricity grids, combined heat and power (CHP), solar photo-voltaics (PV), and energy efficiency. It has made the town centre, housing estates, and old people's homes energy self-sufficient. If the UK grid went down they would have their own heating and electricity year-round. The technologies work in harmony. CHP units generate heating when needed in winter, and electricity along with it when the PV is not working optimally. PV generates a lot of electricity in the summer, when heating is not needed and CHP cannot generate much electricity. Because the use of private wires is so much cheaper than the national grid, the whole package costs fractionally less than the equivalent heating and electricity supply would cost from the big energy suppliers. This ingenuity needs to be compared with what nuclear has to offer. (With thanks to Jeremy Leggett).

**Solarcentury and J C Decaux** supplied Leicester City Council with 750 solar illuminated bus shelters. Once installed, the streetsmart™ shelters will offset over six tonnes of carbon dioxide emissions, helping maintain Leicester City Council's reputation as Britain's first Environment City.

**Hydrogen Partnership** – three Mercedes-Benz Citaro single-decker fuel-cell hydrogen buses began a two-year trial on Route 25 from Oxford Circus to Ilford, east London in October 2005. Mayor Ken Livingstone said the £750,000 buses were the 'greenest, cleanest and quietest ever'. The buses use fuel cell technology to power an electrical engine that can run for 125 miles before refuelling. The only emission is water, which forms into a vapour cloud as it leaves the exhaust. London Hydrogen Partnership (www.lhp.org.uk) is a public-private organisation designed to help bring a hydrogen and fuel cell-based economy in London closer to reality. Members work on infrastructure issues, education and training, as well as implementation of the technology. In this way they hope to set out a route to a cleaner, low carbon future that other cities can follow. London is one of nine European cities taking part in a scheme to reduce greenhouse gas emissions and noise pollution. **Reykjavik, Stockholm, Hamburg, Amsterdam, Stuttgart, Porto and Barcelona – Madrid** has already taken delivery – will get  three buses each.

**Worldwide, city transport initiatives** are using biofuels, compressed natural gas, fuel cells, electric hybrid engines, in Australia, Canada, China, Germany, Japan, Philippines, Thailand and the USA (Green Car Congress). This is mainly but not only in public transport but also in other public service vehicles and delivery vans like UPS for example.

**Biofuels** – British motorists may soon be using petrol blended with ethanol, a fuel made from sugar beet or wheat, and Bio Diesel made from oilseed rape or recycled vegetable oil.  It is part of the Government's fight against climate change (*Independent*, November 2005). Biofuels, made from crops that do not add to carbon dioxide ($CO_2$) emissions, may become an everyday feature of UK road transport, in the biggest shift since unleaded petrol was introduced 15 years ago. Government is drawing up a biofuel obligation, requiring oil companies such as Shell and BP to blend a fixed proportion of biofuels – initially 5 per cent – with all petrol and diesel they sell on garage forecourts.

**Major manufacturers, like Toyota and Honda are developing cleaner engines.** Toyota, with its more economical and low environmental impact cars, like the Prius with dual powered engines, is knocking spots off GM and Ford. With its Range Rovers, Jaguars and SUVs, Ford would better focus on Bill Ford's vision of a few years ago, *'In 25 years, fuel cells could be the predominant way of powering cars.'* Professor David King, the Prime Minister's chief scientific adviser, recently drew attention to Lombardy's proposed ban on new fossil-fuel cars.

**US Mayors** – Bush, slow to be convinced, faces a growing bottom-up rebellion against his environmental denial.  In December 2005, 192 US cities and towns representing more than 40 million Americans, pledged to adopt targets for cutting pollution and gave support to Seattle's Mayor Greg Nickels' nationwide effort to get cities to agree to the Kyoto protocol.

**US States** – In November 2004, nine Northeastern US states signed up to the Regional Greenhouse Gas Initiative (RGGI), a state level emissions capping and trading programme, intended to apply pressure on the federal government by demonstrating that reductions can be achieved without being a signatory of the Kyoto Protocol. Maine, Massachusetts, New Hampshire, Vermont, Rhode Island, Connecticut,

New York, New Jersey and Delaware are participating. California's measures may force big auto manufacturers to introduce cleaner engines.

**Car Clubs may end of our love affair with the private motorcar.** London's first car-free development, a block of flats in Putney, offers a convenient way to cut UK's upward trend in the car population of currently 30 million (*Independent*, 9-1-2006). Andrew Valentine, who set up Streetcar, says they can reduce car use by 70%, the cost of using a car from £2,749pa (AA) to £707pa, the hassle of car ownership *and* $CO_2$ emissions. A study by the Environmental Change Institute shows that 63.5 per cent of car-club members either give up their own cars or don't buy a private vehicle. There are now 30 clubs in UK with around 3,000 members and 100 cars - many more in USA. The DTI supports them. It's a chance to get rid of second cars and save our front gardens.

**Saving lives.** The UK government contributed £2m to help trials of speed limiters, being developed by Oliver Carsten, Professor of Transport Studies at Leeds University, to ensure a vehicle always stays within the speed limit. It is difficult to stick to the limit, or drive to conditions. Few people realise the dramatic difference lower speeds - like slowing from 35 to 30 mph - make to the chances of a pedestrian's survival when hit by a car. As mentioned in Chapter 1, using a digital map of all roads in UK, a satellite will detect a car's location and send a message to the driver that the speed limit is changing and, if necessary, apply the brakes. (*Safety First*, Spring 2003).

## Challenging opportunities:

**Waste: Britain, Dirty Man of Europe,** wastes and dumps a scandalous amount of precious oil-based plastic packaging. At Christmas 2005, according to the *Independent*, Britain discarded more waste than ever before, an estimated three million tons of rubbish - a tenth of the annual total - in a few days. We recycle barely a quarter of jettisoned goods, packaging and uneaten food. The rest is incinerated, sometimes providing power, but polluting the atmosphere, or dumped in landfill sites where heavy metals may seep into the ground. In response, the European Union is threatening legal action. Britain's recycling rates are far lower than in most of old Europe. England's recycling doubled to almost 23 per cent in the past five years; Norway's rate is 68 per cent. Collecting waste, trucking it to and from sites to dumps or recycling pollutes too. It is best to avoid creating waste in the first place and recycle as much as we can in our gardens for compost. **Tesco will recycle your plastic bags.**

*Stop Press:* Belu, a new 'green' company, is producing biodegradable plastic bottles made from corn.

*Government, manufacturers, large retailers and supermarkets need to be pushed; and all of us make better daily choices and lobby!*

**Ethical food purchases in supermarkets are increasing by a staggering 24% per year. Fairtrade** sales rise by over 40%. **Traidcraft** is another example (Ch 12). **Waitrose** won Retailer of the Year 2005 at the RSPCA Alternative Awards, reflecting its commitment to high standards of animal welfare and sustainable fishing. Their partnerships help small family producers of good quality bananas in the Caribbean. They recently introduced a 'Locally Produced' range, to encourage local producers and reduce food miles.

*The challenge for everyone: Much more of this is needed.*

**The organic food market** is likely to rise by about 15 per cent a year to between £2.5bn and £3bn by 2010 (Soil Association). All social classes buy organic food. About 70 per cent of people now buy organic food at least occasionally, though it only accounts for 1 per cent of food sales. Fruit and vegetables are the best-selling organic sectors but dairy and meat are expected to catch up in coming years. Britain, after Germany and Italy, is Europe's third-biggest market for organic food. Organic sales grow much faster than non-organic sales. Sales of organic products through box schemes, farm shops and farmers' markets increased by 33% in 2004. Sales through independent shops rose by 43%.

**Britain's rapidly dwindling farmers cannot supply more than a tiny fraction of this market.** Partly for lack of bold government support, 4,000 organic farms in the UK, with only 4 per cent of total farmland cannot yet meet the demand.

**Local food farming is the most sustainable system.** It is better to supply locally – freshness and food miles. Far from encouraging global sourcing, especially of food, government and international policy needs to discourage global sourcing and encourage largely local sourcing of food throughout the world. This is best for almost every aspect of human life: the environment, local employment, communities, cultures, diversity, our countryside and our spiritual and physical health. Moving livestock all over the country spreads epidemics like TB and Foot and Mouth.

*Berkhamsted Saturday Market:*
*Country Markets stall (ex-WI)*

**Sustainable food production.** Patrick Holden, Soil Association Director, says:

*'... growth in the market is so dynamic. Some supermarkets have experienced a 20 per cent growth over the past year and some of the box schemes have experienced growth of 20 per cent or more. My feeling is that organic and local food market is reaching a tipping point. There are millions and millions of citizens for whom local and organic food purchases have resonance... There are very few people out there now who aren't*

*French olive and cheese stall*

*worried about modern agriculture, climate change, food security, animal welfare, wildlife protection or the maintenance of public health. And those concerns are finding their expression in the market place.'* (Annual Report, December, 2005).

*The challenge for government and citizens: supply most of our food within the UK, locally wherever possible.*

**Mixed local farming is more sustainable but we need to eat far less meat** - another good reason to become largely vegetarian, and eat local wild fish that is not endangered. Meat eating on the US scale is unsustainable. Jonathan Porritt, in his new book (*Capitalism As If The World Matters*), argues that eating less meat would do more for the planet than buying a Prius car!

*'It takes 2kg of feed to produce every kilogram of chicken, 4kg for pork, and at least 7kg for beef. The more meat we eat, the more grain, soya and other feedstuffs we need. So when we hear that the total global meat demand is expected to grow from 209m tonnes in 1997 to around 327m tonnes in 2020, what we have to hold in our mind is all the extra hectares of land required, all the extra water consumed, the extra energy burned, and the extra chemicals applied to grow the requisite amount of feed to produce 327m tonnes of meat.'*

**Elsewhere:**

*'... a sustainable future for the UK depends on securing a thriving rural economy, and that this, in turn, depends on keeping sustainable food production absolutely at the heart of the rural economy. This may come as a bit of a surprise to some conservationists today, but the worst possible outcome for the British countryside and the global environment would be further reform of CAP (Common Agricultural Policy) - ostensibly in the name of 'more environment-friendly farming' - that resulted in more and more farmers going out of business. Which is precisely why we need a much more intelligent debate about food security than the one we're getting at the moment'.*

***The challenge for government, big companies, customers and citizens: we are rapidly completing the destruction of our small, flexible, local, mixed and arable farming and expertise.***

**Countries or regions need to become largely self sufficient in food and energy sourcing.** By 2050, it is predicted, most of the planet's electricity will come from four renewable sources: water, wind, sun and hydrogen. Wind power is the world's fastest growing energy source. Many of these renewable sources can provide cheap power on a small local scale, particularly suitable for poor countries. Huge savings in energy and pollution could be achieved by modifying existing power stations, making them cleaner and more efficient, and reducing waste. This would knock the arguments for toxic and dangerous nuclear power on the head. The costs involved in nuclear generation, security and safety risks, and unresolved problems of waste disposal make nuclear power a 'no-no.' Vested interests need to be persuaded. Rising costs and soaring global demand for oil and gas as countries develop, and the dangerous global politics involved, make it imperative that renewable sources are developed as rapidly as possible.

---

## More Challenges

**Alternative business models**. The John Lewis Partnership, including Waitrose, continues to provide excellence and thrive on a long established employee partnership. Other examples of organisations responding to the desire for real 'ownership' are employee-owned Tower Colliery, the last deep mine in South Wales, and St Luke's advertising agency. The UK's Employee Ownership Index finds that EO companies outperform all the major FT indices over the long term. Scott Bader adopted employee ownership much earlier. Railtrack has transmuted into Network Rail, a new form of not-for-profit corporation, without shares, dividends or investors. This could be a precursor of new forms of company. Current proposals include the Public Interest Corporation, Trustee Enterprise and Limited Liability Partnership (Chris Cook).

**Employee ownership.** USA: Employee Ownership Foundation and ESOP (Employee Share Ownership Programmes) Association promote employee ownership. The association's survey of 1,400 corporate members in 2005, confirms the increase in motivation, productivity and positive benchmarks experienced. 82% of respondents reported ESOP improved motivation and productivity at their company.

UK: Centre for Tomorrow's Company works for legislation to enable new forms of company, corporate responsibility and other benign changes. Job Ownership Limited (JOL) not-for-profit status association of employee and trust owned businesses in the UK promotes employee ownership and expansion of UK's co-owned business by providing fresh thinking and help.

**Servant leadership.** Another positive development, is growing awareness of the need for servant leadership - an ancient idea. Robert Greenleaf Servant Leadership organisation, promoting servant leadership, has corporate members in USA and UK.

---

**Mori polls** consistently confirm that customer and employee satisfaction is related to customer service *and* whether the company is seen as honest and taking its responsibilities to society seriously. People want to work for dynamic, innovative, trustworthy, good corporate citizens. 58% of UK employees believe social and environmental policies are important to 'job satisfaction'(CIPD). Committed people help companies thrive and survive.

**We have a long way to go:** Barry Coates, former Director of the World Development Movement and now Director of Oxfam New Zealand, describes three levels of Corporate Social Responsibility demonstrated by companies:

1. **Saving money though ethical practices** (e.g. recycling, avoiding prosecution)
2. **Ensuring that the company and its products don't get vilified** by taking actions that improve corporate reputation and protect brands.
3. **Acting in a socially and environmentally responsible way** because it's the right thing to do. This is the growth sector!

Increasing numbers of companies actively pursue the first two levels. The problem arises at the third level because the costs of behaving in environmentally and socially responsible ways sometimes impact the bottom line. Then a good leader is punished by the market.

**Two more patterns can be seen**

1. **Big Co buys up Good Co:** McDonald's bought Pret A Manger; Cadbury has bought Green and Black; L'Oreal has bought Body Shop; etc.etc. This may be to learn from them and facilitate transitions but what will the consequences be?
2. **A worrying UK 'short-termist' trend towards bigger dividends** – billions given away that squander capacity to invest in the future.

## Business initiatives are not enough

**We need world citizen leaders in the 21st Century.** Most directors and senior managers are not cynics, just concerned with profit and share value. Most are good people – parents, daughters or sons, family members, partners, friends, neighbours and citizens. Enlightened self-interest and ethical and sustainable businesses are the way to thrive, long term. But because of the global financial system, an enlightened CEO walks a tight rope, risking being sacked by shareholders or the company being taken over. Within the free market framework, most companies only take limited steps. However benign their intentions, it is difficult to survive *and* adopt sustainable and ethical policies when the prime value of free market capitalism and globalisation is to maximise profit and share value at the expense of other values such as human needs, democracy, sustainability and human rights. Only a tiny proportion of companies, like Interface, put sustainability first.

**A level playing field is essential,** to make ethical or sustainable business competitive. Industry wide codes and national and international regulation are needed.

**International institutions, government, both national and regional, need to create a level playing field, provide strategic parameters and funding.** Corporations with government can do much more. Governments need to provide far bolder, more imaginative, strategic measures. Cross-party agreement is essential. Businesses can deliver the necessary innovation if there is the strategic framework for them to do so.

**Progress is far too slow.** Greater pressure on international institutions, regional, national and local government and business is needed.

Citizens and business leaders need to lobby. It is in everyone's interests whether they realise it or not.

The need for a big shift, systemic change, is argued in Chapters 8, 9 and 10.

Ugly buildings and carparks

*Chapter 4*
# Business does great harm

*'The evidence so far is that being ruthless and nasty
actually makes money. We are nice to people, we compensate
them for when we do something wrong.'*
Stelios Haji-Ioannou
commenting on Ryan Air (*Independent* 14-1-2006)

*In the nineteenth century, a dredging company was granted a license
to dredge the shingle at Hallsands, Devon. One night in 1917,
the fishing village fell into the sea.*

**Worst examples:** reported rogue pharmaceutical companies allegedly testing drugs on poor Africans (BBC, R4, *Today*). A dentist friend, returning from Africa, told us well known drinks companies are selling their beverages at lower prices than bottled water in countries where hardly anyone has access to dentistry.

**Is bottling water sustainable?** It costs 10,000 times more to create

64

bottled water than to produce tap water. Huge resources are needed to draw it from the ground, add largely irrelevant minerals, and package and distribute it around the world, thus contributing to global warming. Plastic bottles take 1,000 years to biodegrade, and in industrialised countries, bottled water is no purer or healthier than water from the tap (Earth Policy Institute). Often large quantities of water are used where it is in short supply and desperately needed. It is far more sustainable to invest in making good water supplies available. Water belongs to people, not big companies.

*'We have moved beyond lean and mean into corporate anorexia.'*

Gary Hamel

**It's not the big organisations that suffer from anorexia** – it's employees and the poor of the world. As organisations grow bigger, so does the harm. There is a growing awareness of the costly effects on our health (tobacco, alcohol, food and drinks industries, food sourcing and agribusiness), lifestyles, the environment and how US/Anglo Saxon 'West' is seen by other cultures.

**Big business bears a tremendous responsibility** for its contribution to the development of unhealthy life styles, a culture of always wanting more, constantly promoting dissatisfaction, advertising based on false values, creating wants rather than informing how products meet genuine needs. That's not where the money is. It contributes to a greedy, superficial world in which we have no time.

**We all bear responsibility.** I love mangos but a mango from India or East Africa on our breakfast table will have consumed several hundred times as much energy as it contains getting here. Long distance trawling uses 100 times as much energy as the calories the fish contain; food in our production and distribution system as a whole, uses 10-15 times as much. (Girardet, H, 2004) In most of Africa, water is a scarce resource which people often have to carry for miles for their crops. Yet we buy cut flowers from Kenya, and a 50g pack of lettuce costing 99p requires 50 litres of water to grow and more for washing and processing.

---

**I sat and watched television in Granny's sitting room** in Massachusetts. Mr Rogers telling children *'you are perfect just the way you are'* was lovely; most programmes, punctuated by advertising, were mediocre. I saw an alliance for making money, promoting on one hand, unhealthy lifestyle and unsustainable pollution and, on the other, medicine. Outside, a few people would stroll, fast walk or jog. Most drove. Hired gardeners motor-mowed lawns and spread chemicals. Noisy power boats ruined the tranquility and beauty of the Connecticut river which I viewed from the mountain above. In the village centre, obese people struggled along. I love US people and I felt angry!

---

**Back home,** we sit at computer screens; drive bigger, faster cars seeking 'better value'; get unhealthier; drive to ugly, windowless, noisy sports centres; sit on machines for exercise that would be part of our lives if we walked, cycled safely and led healthier lives. Motor transport dominates our country, ruins towns, pollutes the air we breathe, and creates ever-growing swathes of congested roads. We turn our front gardens into car parks. It's where the money is but it makes for spiritual disease.

**Bigger is not always better.** The driving force of bigger is domination of the market, increased purchasing power, share value and profit. This does not serve the interests of stakeholders: customers, suppliers, employees and community. It creates sudden, constant change and insecurity; often results in poorer service, less human contact, less flexibility, less choice, less rewarding jobs for employees and, often, higher prices. For these reasons, there is opposition to Waterstone's takeover bid for smaller Ottakar's. Ending the recommended retail price made it even harder for small booksellers – yet the average price of a paperback has gone up from £ 5-99 to £8-99 in the past 5 years. Working in the bottom or middle of BIG CO is usually boring and often it is not so nice for customers. If you have a problem, it is often hard to access someone who will sort it with integrity. Top people seem defended behind the ramparts.

**Big money is not better.** US citizens spend on average £3,000 pa per person on health (though nearly half have no health care scheme and what exists weighs heavily on companies); Cuba where everyone is covered, spends £135, has an only slightly lower life expectancy (WHO). The pattern is similar in education and research. Though having enough resources is essential, expensive solutions often create more problems than they solve.

# Big is not always better or cheaper

## Sustainability policy should prioritise support for small

**Creative independent film making in different countries has suffered** from Hollywood buying them up. France insists 50% of films shown are French. Together with the need for celebrity names to enhance profits, diversity and creativity in all the arts is diminished. Big names become boring. Society loses when it is difficult for creative non-celebrities to bring their work to the public. In a healthy society, it should be easier for new talent – all of us to have our day as 'celebs' if we want to.

**Education is too much influenced by Big Co** – for young people and good teachers. In a genuine effort to maintain UK's place in the competitive global economy, education reflects too much the values of top politicians and business – rather than the holistic needs of young people and society. As we know from the experience of our own young people and their good teachers, it's more a preparation for corporate life than for living. Key life skills are not given enough emphasis: how to support one another through emotional difficulties, finding meaning, purpose and becoming truly who we are. Arts, crafts, languages and trades are undervalued. Too few academics understand the importance of processes that involve, and the need to treat students as whole people, not just minds. In Academia, there often is not enough room for emotional and spiritual intelligence. It is an unbalanced model: too much head and yang; not enough yin, heart, body, spirit or wisdom. Celebrity culture, media marketing and advertising foster superficial aspirations and false values and make it harder for young people to handle the identity crisis they often go through in their teens and early twenties.

**Not enough research is done into the <u>causes</u> of major diseases:** cancer, asthma and others, may have their origins in harmful chemicals and air pollution. More than one-third of women in the USA and nearly half the men will have cancer sometime in their lives. Why? It will cause huge distress, anxiety and suffering. But research into causes that could lead to prevention is relatively small – it's not where the money is to be made. **Big money is made in expensive treatment and pharmaceuticals: not health; but disease.**

**Cheap turns out to be very costly.** Brilliant companies like Tesco, drive down prices but at a huge cost – the environment, food miles, jobs, local food supplies, the fabric of our towns and countryside and alienation. Isolation in the countryside is a major problem: half the NHS budget in rural Cambridgeshire is spent on anti-depressants. Our high streets have the same shop names everywhere. Locally grown food supplies have almost gone, though there is a comeback movement.

**Reduced prices from global sourcing do not reflect environmental and social costs.** A quarter of our carbon emissions, excluding international air travel, come from transport. Professors Pretty and Lang estimate the environmental costs of the way we produce and transport food at £3.2bn or £4bn if subsidies are added (Pretty, J and Lang, J). Does it make sense to evaluate renewable energy without costing the damage to the environment resulting from carbon based or nuclear alternatives? Ray Anderson reckons the full cost of a gallon of petrol, in the USA, would be at least $200, including Iraq war costs.

**Business externalises many of the environmental and social costs it creates.** Public services struggle to pick up the pieces and continually need more resources to cope with the pressures; costs grow exponentially. The NHS and Police are under greater stress as alcohol consumption grows and unhealthy lifestyles, food and drinks are promoted. 1 million children cope with an addicted parent (AddAction). Healthy food should be cheaper; the polluter should pay, not the public. Local food shops and markets are often cheaper, especially if we count all the cost of motoring rather than walking. The taxpayer and consumer ultimately pay for the clean-up problems externalised by big companies.

**Externalised costs are not taken into account** in pricing or evaluating alternatives – e.g. sustainable sources of power. The cost of new nuclear power has been underestimated by almost a factor of three and the potential of small-scale renewable energy overlooked – says a new report from the New Economics Foundation. This argues that a broad combination of renewable energy sources, tapped into with a range of micro, small, medium and large-scale technologies, and applied flexibly, could more than meet all of our needs. Better still, this can provide more employment, new jobs, and new access to energy supplies for millions of people around the world who currently lack basics, such as lighting or the ability to cook without inhaling lethal indoor smoke. Current coal and gas fired power stations could be made cleaner and much more efficient too.

**'Ghost Town Britain and the food desert.'** Food in our street markets is poor compared with equivalents in France and Italy. There, fresh high quality food is highly prized by discerning shoppers. Defensive supermarket responses – *'it is not our job to lead public taste', 'our job is to respond to demand', 'shoppers have a choice and they come to us'* – are flawed; the opposite is true! Very little choice is left and the job of responsible companies *is* to lead! To fully understand the effects of supermarkets on our lives, read the New Economics Foundation's report *'Ghost Town Britain'* and the Ecologist's *'Are You Living in a Food Desert?'*

**Agribusiness is harming us in the UK** – and the rest of the world, giving us food lacking quality, taste and nutrition, degrading our soil and opening us up to frequent pandemics. We are disconnected from how food is produced, the earth, the animals, and we are losing traditional knowledge of farming handed down from generations. Prince Charles (interview with the BBC News 27-10-2005) makes the key distinction between agri*business* and agri*culture*:

*'Agriculture must be thought of as a 'culture' and not an industry. We spend far less on food, as a percentage of income, than on the Continent.'*

**Good food, the basis of health and energy, not expensive food, needs to be one of the highest priorities in every culture.**

**Britain now spends £9bn annually on food miles.** As a nation, we are more and more dependent on other countries to put food on our table. Latest figures show Britain now produces 63 per cent of the food we eat, compared with 75 per cent ten years ago. Does this make sense if we want to reduce the $CO_2$ emissions caused by food miles and have fresh local food? Global sourcing, road transport, shipping and aviation contribute over a third of UK's pollution and emissions of carbon dioxide. With threats to global security, we put ourselves in danger by relying so heavily on imports.

Government, food, drinks, retail and advertising industries need to face the fact that the system as it stands is unsustainable. We are just nibbling at the edges rather than making fundamental changes.

Tara Garnett, author of Transport 2000's *Wise Moves*, said:

*'We have developed a global food industry that is hastening the onslaught of climate change. Climate change is not just a power station or car but the food on our plate too.'*

**Large-scale farming receives huge subsidies.** Far better to cap subsidies and concentrate on smaller scale local food production, reducing food miles, good food culture and connecting people again with how food is grown and reared.

**Farmers' incomes, many already extremely low, dropped by nearly a fifth since last year.** Many are leaving the land every year; sons and daughters usually do not replace them. As I write, 3,500 are taking part in a three-day strike action, some pouring their milk on their land. Milk sells at unsustainable prices – much lower than fizzy water and drinks of little or no nutritional value or which are actually harmful. A quarter of all UK cows are lame because of intensive production methods. A campaign for free range milk is beginning. ·

**Loss of heritage and diversity** - we still have 2,000 apple varieties yet only about six relatively bland, tasteless varieties appear on supermarket shelves. Cox's Orange Pippin, the most popular one, needs to be deluged with huge amounts of pesticide unless grown organically. Britain once grew a huge variety of apples. The problem is that customers pay £1-09p per kilo for Cox apples; growers receive around 61p per kilo whereas it costs them 77p. Fruit and vegetables in our supermarkets are about appearance and shelf life rather than freshness, flavour and quality. Prices in Farmers Markets, even in London, are often cheaper.

*Berkhamsted market day*

## Global Consequences

**Global Agribusiness and Supermarkets have devastating effects on rural labour and traditional ways of life** in the developing world. This way, we add to poverty, cause environmental degradation, pollution, salinisation, water shortages and damage the capacity of third world countries to feed themselves. Read Vandana Shiva's website and her BBC Reith Lecture, 2000, about the contribution of globalisation to poverty.

**In India chemical agriculture and genetic engineering are threatening public health** and leading to nutrition decline. Costs of production, involving hybrid and genetically engineered seeds, chemicals and irrigation, increase with every season, pushing farmers into the debt trap and to suicide. (For further information on the impact of agribusiness and WTO policies on women in India, see Women in Agriculture website and chapter 7.)

## The US and Anglo Saxon 'West' exports a crazy way of life the world!

**We are so used to this alienating world, we are barely conscious of how bad it is.** It took a holiday in Tuscany and Umbria with Suzanne, travelling mostly by cheap trains, to realise just how different life can be. I hate unpredictable, stressful UK motorway driving! Meanwhile, our rail travel is the most expensive in Europe and predicted to become more and more crowded. Continental Europe is rapidly expanding strategic high-speed railways. Political vision is lacking thus far in UK.

*Transport, shopping and socialising in Lucca, Tuscany*

*A living system always reacts! Here are a few some examples:*

## Living Systems React

### Good food, local food and local business campaigns.

**Italy may be economically poorer** but it is a country where love of good food is part of the culture as Jamie Oliver has revealed in his *'Jamie's great escape'* TV series. Italians have created the Slow Food, Slow City and Agriturismo! We need more movements like these!

**Small traders in Portobello Road** are empowering themselves and campaigning to save their businesses from extinction. They want the council to create a 'business conservation area' that would keep out the big names that put up property rents to levels they cannot afford. Portobello Road is a delicate eco-system where the small traders and market traders depend on each other. Big brands are beginning to come in. If the small traders' efforts are successful, this would be a wonderful model for other areas. It would need legislation.

**Local Works** is campaigning for a Sustainable Communities Bill to be presented in November 2006. A cross-party group of MPs, including Liberal Democrats, Labour, Conservative and Plaid Cymru first introduced the Bill, originally drafted by the New Economics Foundation, to the House of Commons in March 2003. Its accompanying Early Day Motion (EDM) got 200 signatures. Local Works will keep re-introducing the Bill, as it is anticipated that it will take several years of campaigning to get it passed. It now has 62 national supporting organisations and over 150 MPs have signed the new *Early Day Motion 641* supporting the Bill.

**Local sustainability** means policies that work towards the long-term wellbeing of any given area. That means promoting local economic needs – so money that is spent locally benefits local shops and services, not remote shareholders. Or that the long-term environmental impacts of any planning or economic policies are central to the process of deciding whether they go ahead or not. The Bill's vision of local sustainability also says that the political and social participation and importance of every member of the community should be promoted. An 80-MP, all-party Parliamentary Group for Small Shops is calling for an independent retail regulator, with powers to curb the unchecked growth of the UK's largest store groups (15-2-2006).

**Company law reform.** Friends of the Earth are campaigning to get changes in the Company Law Reform Bill before it goes to parliament. The bill invites directors to *'consider'* their negative impacts. Only shareholders can appeal against companies' actions. FOE want the law changed to require directors to consider and take concrete action to reduce negative impact on communities and the environment wherever they operate. (Further radical ideas in Ch 9)

*Mountain cottage in Cuba*

## Chapter 5
# A Confidence Crisis for Big Business

## We are falling out of love with big business.

*This chapter tries to make sense of the further harm big business is doing and how our eyes are opening: the full extent of the effect on the poor and developing world, the power they have, the effect on democracy, how they dominate global institutions and how we are falling out of love with them.*

**Recently two women friends came to lunch.** They told me women are tumbling out of big corporations 'with their eyes open'. They dislike the toxic culture, the politics and feel their values are compromised. Women in particular, many extremely able leaders, don't leave business; they do something more meaningful, starting their own businesses or move into the NGO sector. They referred me to an article:

'... *many corporations don't hold enough promise, enough room to mature, to evolve, to be the sorts of places that successful women want to run.'*

*Something Toxic on the Ceiling*, Liz Ryan, *Time*, November 2003

## A confidence crisis for big business

**A succession of financial scandals has affected thousands of people throughout the world.**

Recent scandals include Enron, Parmalet, WorldCom, Andersen (relationships between auditing and consulting functions of consultancies that lack integrity, auditing fees dwarfed by those from consulting), and Boeing's ethical lapses in defence contracting which ultimately sent two executives to jail. Reports of business malpractice in USA, EU and UK continue. Well respected companies lose credibility, like Shell overplaying its reserves and its questionable record in Nigeria; BP's alleged involvement in human rights abuses in West Papua, private lobbying in Washington against a senator's new US bill to cut $CO_2$ emissions, BAT's shifting its marketing of cigarettes to Asia. All these examples dent confidence in Corporate Social Responsibility (CSR). **In the worst cases, the whole world economy and almost everyone suffers.**

**The perception of 'fat cat' greed continues.** UK directors' pay climbed three times faster than average earnings in 2003. Reports of directors bolstering their own pensions, whilst those of ordinary employees suffer, continue – e.g. Rover and the Phoenix Four. A large proportion of corporate profits, particularly in USA, are held in tax havens. The Economist reported Rupert Murdoch paid no tax in the UK since 1987 on his £1.4 billion profit because of the way he uses the global system to avoid tax.

*Corruption in and greed in the 'West' and Africa mirror each other.*

**Tobacco is a killer industry.** In England, 364,000 patients are admitted to NHS hospitals each year due to diseases caused by smoking. Recent estimates are that half the teenagers who now smoke will die from diseases caused by tobacco if they continue. Between 1950 and 2000 six million Britons, 60 million people worldwide, died from tobacco-related diseases. In the UK each year, about 114,000 are killed by smoking, one fifth of all UK deaths, and over 11,000 by passive smoking. Worldwide, almost 5 million pa die prematurely as a result of smoking. On current trends, this will rise to 10 million within 20 years. Spend on prevention is paltry compared with advertising. (Source ASH)

British American Tobacco, as responsible as any tobacco company can be, do a lot of good – treat their workers on tobacco plantations well, support ecological diversity and do many charitable works. **They need a strategy to get out of tobacco and set an example!** A black friend compared this with 'nice' slave owners justifying continuing to be in the slavery business. Getting out responsibly is complicated. They need a long-term strategy to do so. Everything would conspire to support them.

**Alcohol accounts for four times as many deaths as drugs**, which attract far more political attention and resources. Deaths in England and Wales caused by alcohol rose by from 5,525 in 2000 to 6,544 in 2004 - an 18.4% increase. Other research - which covers relevant types of cancers, strokes, heart disease and dementia, as well as accidents, suicides and assaults - probably provides a more accurate picture. These studies estimate the figure to be over 30,000 deaths a year (Source Alcohol Concern). Alcohol is more complicated than tobacco - it depends how people use it but marketing and advertising bear a heavy responsibility. Alcopops played an early major part in the current problem with young people's drinking and disorder.

**It is interesting to reflect that tobacco is a deadly product. In excess, so are alcohol and marijuana.** The first two industries have created aristocracy, are establishment and big sources of tax revenue. Marijuana is illegal and, back garden or attic production aside, involves persecuted poor producers, street 'retailers', military interventions and no tax revenue. Think about it cynically! Bolivian President Evo Morales, former coca farmer, says no to drugs but yes to coca, which is part of their culture and agriculture.

## The problem with CSR and business in the community

Much CSR is about good work in the community, e.g. community-minded business supporting the arts and giving to good causes. However the core business may do harm. Go-Ahead Buses run a lot of good community projects. But they *also* address the core problem: pollution caused by current engines. They invest in vehicles with cleaner engines and experiment with hydrogen cell engines.

**CSR is viewed with scepticism,** more 'spin' than substance – 'greenwashing'. Are their expensive conferences group denial and celebration of looking good rather than doing good, profitable business and avoiding harm?

**Real CSR means radical change:** making a business case for acting in a socially and environmentally responsible way because it's the right thing to do; getting out of harmful and undemocratic activities; cleaning up one's act completely and developing markets for new or improved products and services that are sustainable. This is complex as companies with harmful business at the core, also do good, providing employment, development opportunities and much besides. That is misused as an excuse.

## Big Co, EU and USA and Global Institutions do great harm

**EU and US subsidies threaten the livelihoods of millions of farmers everywhere, especially in the developing world.** Subsidies encourage over-production. The huge surpluses they create are dumped on international markets, undercutting and ruining farmers in many of the world's poorest countries – food aid does so too. (Oxfam, October 2002). EU's Common Agricultural Policy has improved but still subsidises rich farmers and corporations and poor alike. Cows earn twice as much as the poorest people in the world. A cap is needed so that only small farmers are subsidised.

**Smaller countries that find it hard to compete** and poor countries need support. The recent decision of the EU, supported by Britain, to 'reform' its sugar regime will lead to a devastating impact in the Caribbean sugar producing countries by reducing the price they receive for sugar by 36% by 2009, starting with the first cut taking place in July 2006. Thus all six Caribbean countries with sugar industries, Trinidad & Tobago, St. Kitts Nevis, Jamaica, Barbados, Belize and Guyana, are affected. It is estimated that in total they will lose nearly US$100 million per annum in vital export earnings.

**To create a more sustainable worl**d, the focus needs to be on supporting the sustainable: local and organic food production, crops required for bio fuels, support for smaller poor countries and smaller farmers everywhere. **Big Co** can look after itself.

**Current World Trade proposals would open up public services to international companies.** The EU is trying to force poor countries to hand over their public utilities, education and health services to corporations. It is not working. Maximising international trade undermines local production and increases the pollution from transportation. Global institutions that are not inclusive and ignore the interests of ordinary people face protest on the streets; their conferences become unwelcome to potential host cities. So long as trade is unfair, **we invite mass migration** of people trying to escape poverty.

**Trans National Corporations** (TNCs) need to be controlled and financial markets require regulation. Big business is not democratically accountable. However benign, business works within an unsustainable system.

**Global Institutions: the whole global framework for business needs reforming.** Global institutions such as the IMF, World Bank and the World Trade Organisation (WTO), whose dominant value is promoting free market capitalism, the reach and power of Trans National

Corporations (TNCs) and maximising profit and share value need to be reformed or replaced. The simple truth is they are undemocratic and their policies have largely enriched a privileged minority at the expense of the vast majority of human beings. Equally important, they are ecologically unsustainable.

**Trade rules established by the unaccountable and unrepresentative WTO are not fair.** They are heavily biased in favour of the richest countries and TNCs. The benefit of free trade to ordinary people, as opposed to rich elites in poor countries is unproven. The odds are stacked against the Third World. For example, under the GATTS rules, poor countries are forced to open their markets to imports of heavily subsidised produce from the West, thus ruining poor farmers, many of whom are already living on a dollar a day.

## Big Co threatens democracy

**The economies of many trans-national corporations** (TNCs) are larger than medium-sized nations. Democratic national governments or regions such as the EU dare not introduce sustainable policies that put them at a competitive disadvantage. National governments have to woo TNCs in their desire to create favourable conditions for investment and employment in their countries. TNCs exert great influence on politicians, global institutions and the current world free trade policies. It is these unfair trade policies and free market capitalism, which arguably are having the most damaging effect on the impoverished, poor countries and the environment.

**The connections of big business to politicians are too close.** The contributions of corporations to the campaign costs in US Presidential, Senate and House of Representatives elections are enormous. Generally, the presidential candidate with the largest campaign fund is elected. Reports on how the Bush administration and global institutions are staffed or influenced by former members of global oil, chemical and agribusiness corporations reveal a shameful threat to democracy and justice.

**The threat to democracy**, when the media gets too big, is illustrated by Fox, Murdoch etc and allegedly right wing Disney's gaining control of distribution by buying up Miramax and refusing distribution of Michael Moore's Fahrenheit 9/11. It fails.

**The Asia-Pacific Partnership on Clean Development and Climate.** The first ministerial gathering, in Sydney in January 2006, included three of world's biggest polluters US, China and India, plus Japan, South Korea and Australia. Financial incentives such as the European Union's Emissions Trading Scheme, rewarding companies for reducing their carbon output, are not envisaged. US Energy Secretary, Samuel Bodman, believes that without targets or financial incentives, coal, gas and energy companies *are* capable of reducing harmful emissions. Technology, developed and exported to the growing economies of Asia, can reduce emissions without binding targets as contained in the Kyoto treaty. He advocates nuclear power too - a dangerous, costly option I believe which needs to be strongly opposed by citizens.

**Environmentalists view this as a 'counter-Kyoto' alliance** - a rival to the Kyoto process, a diversion to avoid signing up to binding targets like those in the Kyoto Protocol.. They suspect it is basically designed to help western energy companies into burgeoning Asia. They doubt companies or governments will adopt these technologies if they cost more than conventional systems. 'Governments have to set the rules by which private companies operate,' says Erwin Jackson of the Australian Conservation Foundation.

*The 'either/or' approach is unhelpful. The sensible answer is: we need 'both and.'*

**The connections of Bush, Cheney and colleagues** to Esso, Halliburton and arms manufacturers are well known. Bush's business connections and meeting with the Saudi Arabian royal family including the snip of his introductory remarks about the 'haves and the have mores' were exposed in Michael Moore's Fahrenheit 9/11. US democracy is a deeply flawed system.

**We have to be realistic and acknowledge the dark side:** greed, empire building, corruption, huge sums spent on lobbying, white-collar crime, dirty tricks, cover-ups, spin, double talk, lip service, conflicts of interest, wide gaps between declared policy and reality etc. Big business is too powerful, exercises too much influence over politicians and national and global institutions. Relationships between politics and business are too close and undermine integrity and democracy.

*We need constantly sceptical and probing citizens, NGOs and media.*

**Steady pressure is needed on businesses that fail ˙ to respond.** Ultimately, organisations promoting harmful products or harming communities, face increasing protests, costly lawsuits, loss of reputation and decline. Better to face it. Denial and 'green washing' won't work.

## Steady pressure on businesses

- **Wal-Mart faces prosecution** from Maryland State with a health care bill. Wal-Mart, the world's largest retailer, held out as a model in unaware nineties literature – 'Built to last!' (Collins J. and Porras J) – owned by the world's richest family, is now subject to major adverse publicity. Wal-Mart allegedly hands out state food vouchers to employees. Their stores are popular for their low prices, but critics accuse them of achieving success by denying workers' rights. A California court found Wal-Mart broke a state law requiring employers to give staff an unpaid 30-minute lunch break if they worked more than six hours and ordered it to pay $172m (£99m) in compensation to workers refused lunch breaks. More than 100,000 Wal-Mart employees in California would be eligible for compensation.

- **Canada's Supreme Court** recently upheld the British Columbia government's right to seek damages of £4.8bn for 50 years of health care provision, from tobacco companies including Imperial Tobacco, Philip Morris, the group owning Marlborough, and Rothmans. Other provinces are likely to follow suit. Coca Cola faces massive protests in India. McDonald's profits are suffering and it has faced massive adverse publicity. Following suits against tobacco companies, McDonald's, Burger King, Kentucky Fried Chicken and Nabisco face obesity lawsuits. Action Aid's report *'Power Hungry; six reasons to regulate global food corporations'* argues that multinationals such as Nestlé, Unilever, Monsanto, Parmalat, Cargill and Wal-Mart have gained control of the global food chain – all the way from seed to supermarket shelf and are threatening the livelihoods of hundreds of thousands of poor farmers and undermining their basic rights. Action Aid also alleges that some of Tesco's £2bn profit announced in March 2005 is made at the expense of appalling working conditions for thousands of women workers in South Africa who grow the fruit that ends up on Tesco's shelves.

- **At last, after 20 years, vending machines in schools, offering ill health to our children, are being replaced.** Many of the products sold cause hyperactive behaviour in the classroom as well as obesity and who knows what harm to children's future health, cost to the nation, taxpayers, you and me. Jamie Oliver with his TV programmes, forced out bad vending machine offerings and poor quality food, after years of culpable neglect. He got the extra money and taught dinner ladies to cook good food. Government acted at last – the battle continues ...

*This is how the living system works – in these cases, too slowly.*

*James Hannaway at the Rex Cinema, with a group of children on a birthday visit*

**Instead, Big Co could learn faster.** I asked James Hannaway, who succeeded against the odds as co-creator of Berkhamsted's amazing, restored Art Deco cinema (Rex Cinema – 'probably the most beautiful cinema in Britain'), *'What is the secret of your success?'* His people like to come to work and, with its wonderful programme, it is a success, even for a children's birthday celebration. His simple answer was: *'We learn.'*

*World War I memorial
in West Kirby*

## Chapter 6
# Loss of Confidence in Political Leadership

## The politics of the playground on the world stage in deadly form

*'This is an impressive crowd – the haves and the have mores. Some
people call you the elite – I call you my base.'*

George W Bush

Today I read a headline:

*'US tells Hamas: renounce terror or lose $400M of aid'*

It reminded me of when I was 10. A big boy tried and failed to bully me in
the school playground. Being very big, he simply sat on me but somehow I
managed to get out. We ended up friends.

**Bullying on the international stage has deadly consequences for
millions of people, and the ultimate potential to kill all of us.**

**We might as well face up to what it is to be human.** *Because of the 'Beast Within'* – our nature – and the way people are damaged, *we need structured justice to prevent injustices occurring* (Peter Challen). We also need organisations like the United Nations and the International Court of Justice, police, regulation, law, courts, watchdogs, a relentlessly inquisitive media and active citizens who participate, lobby and demonstrate. It has taken centuries of violent conflict to establish law and order in the most advanced countries. Much more recent is the quest for international law and order. Now, events are forcing us to see that it is becoming imperative that we act, not from the Beast Within but from awareness of our nature and 21st Century principles.

**We have a good Prime Minister and government team.** Most people, going into politics have good intentions and want to make a difference and create a better world. But they can be a danger to humanity. We are all damaged to some extent and top leaders in politics and business are no exception. History shows the way top people are damaged has massive repercussions, affecting millions or even billions of people. The responsibilities of top leaders are enormous and the toxic environment they work in can corrupt or destroy them. As time runs out, they feel a desperate need to leave a historic legacy. That distorts judgement. It is hard to stay balanced, living in a circle of celebrities, often needy for attention, wealth and power. People can become even more damaged in that environment. It is not helped by UK's drink culture, reflected in the sixteen pubs in the Palace of Westminster – one of the few work places with drink available! Too much advocacy is dangerous when wise, complex decisions are needed – and bad for health, as one of my friends tells me.

*Politicians, often schooled in adversarial behaviour – in advocacy, law and journalism – may have little understanding of servant leadership or how to co-create 'joined up' change to which people on the ground are committed.*

**The House of Commons,** haunted by the spirit of Charles the First with his 'Divine Right of Kings', and beheaded like obdurate Marie-Antoinette, has as its model a nearby ecclesiastical building where it first met, with an altar where the 'Speaker' sits and pews for the rowdy choirboys facing each other. It is not the symbolic circle we need today, found almost everywhere else. Its history and ridiculous, antiquated customs are obstacles. The artificial process of addressing questions to the Speaker is nothing like a modern process of conversation (Chapter 10). It is difficult to 'call out' someone who is unfit because of inebriation, or not being truthful. All the performance and drama get in the way of sensible discussion, truth and reaching wise and fully informed judgements. Balanced, complex decisions about the most vital issues require listening, really hearing many different, contrary views and taking them into account. Michael Meacher says, 'truth and trust' are essential.

Tony Blair still believes he was right to act against the opposition of half the citizens, called 'subjects.' **He used the Royal Prerogative to go to war**. Bush needed permission from Congress. In the face of such opposition, is a leader of a democracy justified when there is no actual immediate or probable threat to the nation?

**Rather than waging an illegal war, leaders would better put their own houses in order** – address *un*sustainability, injustice and poverty in their own countries and examine their own part in global issues.

*The default process in politics is __group think__, suppression of truth, defence, denial, obfuscation and bearing down on opposition.*

Notice the word Government *'Whips.'* The very opposite is needed: getting to truth, understanding other ways of seeing the world and reaching common ground. The latest example is obfuscation over whether Britain colluded in the flights and re-fuelling stops at UK airports in US transportation of terrorist suspects to various countries for *'exceptional rendering'* – an extraordinary, evasive term reminiscent of the slaughterhouse. The Oxford Council on Good Governance argues there is big cover up and in December 2005 called for massive demonstrations against US Secretary of State Condoleezza Rice in Germany, Belgium, Romania and Ukraine. Was UK's former Ambassador to the UN, Sir Jeremy Greenstock muzzled, his memoirs allegedly not yet authorised by the Foreign Secretary?

*In business too, the default process is __group think__, suppressing truth, defence, denial and punishing opposition.*

A scandalous example has just been exposed. In many much used types of aircraft, toxic gas on flight decks frequently threatens safety and passenger health. (*Observer*, 25-2-2006).

*It is part of the human psyche and happens at home too.*

———————————oooooooOooooooo———————————

**The experience of the war in Iraq has shaken confidence in democracy and force as a means of addressing global problems.** Many people question the efficacy of violent force. George Bush speaks of *'freedom loving peoples.'* Is *freedom to make money* what he really has in mind?

**Deaths of US soldiers have well exceeded 2,000.** *Lancet* estimated that 100,000 Iraq civilians have died in the conflict, though it is claimed that no records have been kept by the US military. Others estimate some 25,000 civilian deaths. In late October 2005, the US military revealed that some 26,000 Iraqis have died or been injured in the insurgency since January 2005. A recent estimate put the number of Iraq citizens kidnapped at 5,000. Is it that Iraqi deaths and kidnappings matter less than those of allied soldiers and civilians? That does not take account of all the injuries and the traumatic effects of the war on soldiers and civilians alike, including children. The attack and siege of Falluja (a city of over 250,000) April to November 2004, forcing most residents to flee and many becoming homeless, caused 616 civilian deaths according to Iraq Body Count. The health situation is dire in Iraq, once one of the most prosperous developing countries. After 12 years of UN-imposed economic sanctions and two Gulf Wars, many of Iraq's 27 million people have become impoverished. As many experienced experts warned, Iraq is in chaos and suicide attacks are increasing, though following parliamentary elections in December 2005, it was hoped suicide attacks would subside.

**Before the invasion of Iraq,** the Kuwait war and UN sanctions had catastrophic effects on hundreds of thousands of children, stunting their growth, health, education and development. The education system collapsed. Charles Sennott's shocking article (*Boston Globe*, 25-1-1999), spoke of:

*'Iraq's lost generation – stunted by malnourishment, trapped in ignorance, orphaned by war, and forgotten by the world.'*

Ramsey Clark, former US Attorney General, founder of the International Action Center (IAC), waged a long campaign to end the United Nations economic sanctions: he argued they caused widespread human suffering and the death of 700,000 Iraqi civilians, although Iraq had fully complied with all of the conditions imposed at the end of the 1991 Gulf War, and USA bullied the UN Security Council into renewing the sanctions every two months.

**However obnoxious Saddam Hussein's regime may have been**, it was an illegal war that contravened the UN charter. Not supported by the UN, USA flouted international law, and went to war on a false justification about weapons of mass destruction. The people of the United States, the British people and Parliament were misled through lack of *'due diligence.'* Unilateral action by the US, supported by Britain and a few other countries, misleadingly described as 'The Allies', undermined the UN, our best hope for future peace. Cheney and Bush could be war criminals. It is hardly surprising that USA opposes an International Court of Justice.

**Harry Patch, at the age of 108**, one of the last conscripts of WW1, is vehemently opposed to war. He says:

*'War is useless. You lose a lot of lives, for what? How is it ended? Over a table. They should have done that before they lost all those lives at Passchendaele. If you declare war, it's simply the government given license to go to a foreign country and commit murder. That's all war is – murder.'*

Harry Patch, interviewed in the *Radio Times*, November 2005

Not hating Germans, he tried to wound rather than kill. He hated the Kaiser who started the war.

**Aggressive wars are started by leaders who do not fight them.** Almost always, they are lost. They traumatise and blight the happiness of wives, mothers and families: many service people come back mentally ill; some commit suicide.

A friend showed us a picture of herself as a beautiful young open-faced woman; her husband was never well after coming back from Suez and died of cancer when only 47. Still beautiful at 74, she does not have an adequate pension and has to work.

There are parallels in how cost-cutting business leaders bear down most heavily on employees.

**The cost of the Iraq war to the US was estimated to reach $204.6 billion** by the end of fiscal year 2005 (National Priorities Organisation). The MoD recently disclosed that the Iraq war and its aftermath would have cost the UK about £3.1bn by the end of March 2005. Would the billions spent on the war, benefiting arms companies and support industries, be better spent investing in sustainability, education, health and the alleviation of poverty in their own countries and in the Third World? *Of course!*

**G8 countries' spending on arms exceeded $1trillion in 2004** whilst they spent $79 billion on development aid. USA spends $455.3 billion on arms and $19bn on aid; UK $47.4bn and $7.8bn (OECD Departmental Assistance Committee). Analysts estimate $50billion in additional annual funding could achieve the Millennium Development Goals (World Watch report 2005). Cynic me notes a lot of money is to be made in war (Bernard Shaw's *Major Barbara* again). USA followed by UK, is the largest arms supplier, much of the armaments going to developing countries.

**The 20th century accounted for 95% of over 120,000,000 war deaths since 1700**, 40 million from 1945 to year 2000. At the close of the century, despite 'precision weapons' demonstrated on TV, over 95% of these deaths were civilian compared with 52% in the 1960s. Startling evidence is that those who start wars rarely win (Peace Pledge Union). The Vietnam War – costing the United States 58,000 lives and 350,000 casualties, resulted in between one and two million Vietnamese deaths – was lost.

**Many believe the Iraq war has unleashed an even greater threat to the 'West'.** *'War on terror'* is unlikely to work, does not think through the long-term future or deal with underlying issues that breed violence. Amongst these are the difficulties of young people in Muslim communities in Britain – the alienation of young Muslims who feel without hope, as they see an assault on Islam through cynical foreign policies of US, UK and other EU countries throughout the centuries, but especially since the end of WW1, and injustice towards Palestine.

**Identity Cards**, taking us back to WW2, are probably inappropriate for today. LSE says the 'best case scenario' for the cost of the ID card scheme is £10.6bn, about £170 per card and passport; 'worst case' £19.2bn. Spending on remedying the underlying causes of insecurity – creating opportunities, education, universities, research and sustainability, especially in UK's most disadvantaged communities and poor countries – would do more for security than oppressive measures going back to Wartime Britain.

*War diverts attention and resources from fundamental issues.*

————————————oooooooOoooooo————————————

**National Debt.** Here are some interesting extracts from John F Ince's article, *America's Debt Time Bomb*, in AlterNet, posted December 1, 2005.

*'When President Bush took office in 2000, the projected surplus for the US government for the next decade was approximately $5 trillion. By fiscal year 2005, the surplus was entirely gone and the annual domestic deficits were at record levels, somewhere in the range of $350-450 billion depending on whose estimates you use. This is the most radical reversal of government finances in US history. Today the national debt is approximately $7.9 trillion, and growing by over a billion a day.*

*In the last 25 years, America has gone from the world's largest creditor nation to the world's largest debtor nation ... Should we continue to run current account deficits comparable to those now prevailing, the net ownership of the US by other countries and their citizens a decade from now will amount to roughly $11 trillion.*

*While military expenditures go unquestioned in Congress, funding is being cut for education, environmental protection, sustainable energy programs and many other programs that arguably will have a more profound effect on the strength and economic competitiveness of our country. Increasingly, the battleground of modern international conflict will be in the global marketplace, rather than in the military sphere. China's need for energy and other resources will ultimately place its national requirements on a collision course with those of the US and other Western nations.*

*Sooner or later, America must begin paying off its debts, and its binge of borrowing must come to an end. If our leaders continue to ignore the problem, we will all suffer the consequences.'*

Are we in UK now doing the same, albeit on a smaller scale?

————————————oooooooOoooooo————————————

**Can politicians be trusted?** People see through our so-called 'ethical foreign policy'. Reading Mark Curtis's books is a revelation! Obviously, of course, Tony Blair would support Bush's war – it's the pattern of British foreign policy since the end of WW2 and previously the repressive, racist British Empire. Only Harold Wilson stood up to President Kennedy, saying 'no' to the Vietnam War.

In his well-researched books (Curtis, M, 2003/2004), he estimates British foreign policy from the end of WW2 has been directly or indirectly responsible for around 10 million deaths worldwide. New Labour, since achieving power, ceaselessly makes extraordinary claims about the morality of their foreign policies, wanting to be a 'force for good in the world." Yet never in British history has there been such a gap between government claims and reality, he argues.

**Revelations of US political corruption reached new heights** recently when Republican congress leader Tom DeLay, resigned. He and long-term lobbyist Jack Abramoff pleaded guilty to fraud charges. Tom DeLay with two others stood accused of laundering $190,000 (£109,000) in corporate donations for distribution to Republican candidates and the Texas Legislature in the 2002 state campaign. Texas state law forbids the use of corporate money for political campaigns. Corruption like this is not new.

*Close links between top politicians, big business and celebrities add to popular cynicism.*

**People see through the inconsistency of US (and UK) foreign policy**, interfering and supporting corrupt, tyrannical, killer rulers, like Saddam Hussein and others in Latin America. Commercial interests, oil, political interests, not ethics, take primacy and explain the lack of even-handedness in the conflict between Israel and Palestine and the US government's unfair treatment of Cuba. Cuba, in many ways an enlightened little country, has excellent health, education services and medical research, support for poor countries, bottom-up democracy, and exemplary sustainable local, organic food production in Havana (Cuba Si and Cuba Organic Support Group). Bush, acting on a message from God, apparently, went to war in Iraq on behalf of big business and opportunities for the likes of Halliburton.

**Tony Blair, with the best of intentions, misled the nation.** Did he have a 'divine right' to take the nation to war without the formal approval of a fully informed parliament and with many citizens opposing war, because of his conviction that it was right? Expensive 'hog-washing' inquiries, commissions and dramas delay, distract and precipitate the death and resignation of good people.

*Denial, again, is a major flaw in human behaviour.*

**The underlying thrust of Tony Blair's well-intentioned Africa Commission**

seems like neo-colonialism, implanting Western approaches, seeking opportunities for business rather than supporting African people in creating their own solutions, including grass roots initiatives. The dire situation in Africa today, though rooted in a colonial legacy, a difficult terrain and climate, is substantially due to Western interference, unfair terms of trade, including high tariffs, dumping subsidised food produce, a huge debt and interest burden, and an arms trade centred in London (Dowden, R, 2005). Fair trade – not charity, interference and aid – will help Africans fundamentally transform the situation. Promises and years of grand summits have produced little so far.

**Loss of trust in political institutions** to bring about change, results in declining membership of political parties. 51% voted in UK's 2001 election. In May 2005, Labour won a majority of 67 with only 35 per cent of the votes cast and the support of just 22 per cent of the electorate and it did not reflect their wishes. People are profoundly alienated. Instead, they join NGOs and single-issue groups, march on the streets and join demonstrations. They use the internet to get to the truth, campaign, express their views in large numbers and lobby government ministers, parliamentary representatives and international organisations.

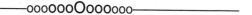

**Reforming Democracy** – in the UK, we have one of the best democracies but there is considerable scope for improvement. Charter 88, supported by Helena Kennedy QC, was launched in 1988:

---

### The Charter 88 campaign

- Human Rights Act (enacted 1998) incorporating freedom from discrimination, except religious.
- Freedom of Information Act (now enacted)
- Open government
- Devolution and decentralisation of power (extended in limited form to Scotland and Wales; rejected in the North by referendum)
- Reform of the House of Commons
- A democratic second chamber (limited)
- Proportional representation
- An independent judiciary
- A written constitution - a new contract between citizens and those who govern in our name

---

**Progress has been achingly slow.** There is huge resistance to letting go of power, secrecy and privilege. All kinds of excuses are made to delay or hold on, resist a voting system that would bring about a House of Commons matching the electorate's votes. Political patronage of cronies and financial supporters continues in the House of Lords and honours system. The Freedom of Information was watered down, enacted slowly, obstructed and a battle to implement. Government resists telling the truth and admitting mistakes.

**17 years later, Power to the People,** chaired by Baroness Helena Kennedy QC, now a Labour peer, tells the parties they are 'killing' politics.

- What is needed is a responsive electoral system for the House of Commons, House of Lords and local councils to replace the first-past-the-post system 'to ensure that all votes count by having some influence on the final outcome of an election.'
- 70 per cent of the House of Lords should be elected by a 'responsive electoral system'.
- Parliament should be able to initiate legislation, launch inquiries and act on petitions.
- Voting and candidacy age should be reduced to 16.
- A commission should encourage women, ethnic minorities, people on lower incomes, young people and independents to stand.
- £10,000 should be the limit on individual donations to parties.
- Power should be decentralised from central to local government.
- Curbs are needed on the powers of party 'whips'.
- There should be more powers for select committees to hold ministers to account.
- There should be tighter rules on plurality of media ownership.

It warns politicians they must learn.

*'Politics and government are increasingly in the hands of privileged elites as if democracy has run out of steam. Too often citizens are being evicted from decision-making – rarely asked to get involved and rarely listened to. As a result, they see no point in voting, joining a party or engaging with formal politics.'* (*Independent*, 27-2-2006)

**The Monarchy is part of the problem** and also needs to be reformed, slimmed down and updated. **The honours system needs reforming.** It acknowledges genuinely wonderful people. It is also archaic and some people still buy their way in by party donations and loans, or get honours just by being there. It is undemocratic, harking back to the British Empire and its supporting class hierarchy. Benjamin Zephaniah just could not accept an honour reminding him of an oppressive imperial past. He spoke his mind plainly.

*People in power need the courage to address these issues willingly or they will be forced.*

ooooooo**O**ooooooo

**The toxic dynamics of UK politics and media are linked** and work against good political leadership and government. At its worst, the adversarial system in the House of Commons and the media is puerile. Pugilistic dramas in the House of Commons, between the media and politicians, dragging in personal lives, militate against honesty, integrity and a sensible constructive dialogue. It was typified by the battle between the former BBC Director General, Greg Dyke, and Alastair Campbell over the alleged sexing up of the case for the war against Iraq and a tragic suicide. Charles Kennedy is the latest casualty of toxic culture, drink and verbal violence.

**The Media colludes:** they inflate with inaccuracy. Interviewers constantly ask: *'Who's to blame?'* a silly, unhelpful question. *'Responsibility'*, a more useful word, is always shared. Interviewers try to trap politicians into admitting failure or *'giving in'* or *'doing a u-turn'* instead of asking more useful questions. Immature politicians claim credit falsely and take petty swipes at each other like young children. Interviewers should 'interrupt' this ridiculous behaviour.

**It is sensible to be flexible** – change your mind, make concessions to find common ground, do a u-turn or change direction when new events, information or points of view make this the intelligent thing to do. Leaders would set a good example if they admitted mistakes and changed their minds. Being consistent about anything but integrity makes no sense.

*It is insanity not to change your mind when you have new information and need a solution that has the widest support.*

It is primitive and foolish to subject leaders to this treatment if we expect them to act wisely. A punishing system puts leaders, whose wise judgement is vital, under excessive strain. It makes the job intolerable for anyone without an incredibly tough hide and adds to the stress of a workload that strains the strongest constitution.

**Being a bruiser with the ability to deal with the media** seems to be the main criterion for effective political leadership, rather than understanding of the issues, passion for the job, integrity and effective communication. Estelle Morris, now elevated to the House of Lords and voted by MPs and peers as minister of the year in July 2003, was replaced after her honest dealings with a macho media. She was praised by heads, teachers and civil servants. A colleague said she was widely seen as one of the most decent and highly regarded people in government.

*'She's the kind of person who gives politicians a good name.' 'She had an ability to communicate and to understand exactly what heads and*

*teachers needed that was second to none. She actually wanted to do what was the best for children'.*

Dame Jean Else, her former head

*'Frankly, it is very noticeable that the people put in as being the hard ministers are all male. Both are old Labour 'bruisers'. The implication is that Estelle is just a mere woman and can't do it very well, which is offensive. Frankly, if two thirds of the Cabinet were examined on the basis of whether or not they could do the job, there would be a hell of a lot of sackings tomorrow.'*

Gwyneth Dunwoody, Commons Transport Committee Chair.

**Women find a very different atmosphere in the House of Lords,** far more conducive to rational discussion. A powerful coalition of female Labour ministers warned Tony Blair and Gordon Brown against pushing the party towards a 'macho' policy agenda. Senior figures are insisting Labour's 'renewal' programme will fail unless it includes more female-friendly policies (Independent reported 28-10-2005).

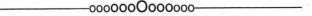

**An underlying issue is an outdated approach to leadership,** essentially patriarchal, conflicting with best thinking about leadership and bringing about successful change. Tony Blair's leadership seems top down. Some say his substantial majority enabled him to exercise 'quasi dictatorship'. There has been a pronounced lack of transparency. There have been many examples – restructuring police forces, local health bodies, primary care trusts, reducing the range of services from district nursing to physiotherapy and sourcing them from the private sector, arguably more expensive.

**There is far more open consultation today than there used to be.** White papers are published on the internet and anybody can respond. But not many people know about or respond to these invitations. There is disbelief or uncertainty about whether it is real consultation or a cosmetic exercise, e.g. the Tomlinson Report on Education and the resulting Education White Paper.

*Politicians do not understand the difference between consulting and involving and engaging people!*

**The process is the problem** – see Chapter 10.

## Positive steps

If you want to fight for what you care about and improve our democracy, there are many websites you can use to keep you informed and enable you to put pressure on government. Amongst these are US International Action Center (IAC), Peace Pledge Union, One World, Amnesty International, Charter 88, New Politics Network - currently campaigning for an elected Second Chamber, and a form of proportional representation - also supported by the Electoral Reform Society. The Armed Forces (Parliamentary Approval for Participation in Armed Conflict) Bill, requiring the Prime Minister to gain approval from Parliament before going to war for receives its second reading. The House of Lords' Constitution Committee is examining the use of the Royal Prerogative, with particular regard to the Government's ability to go to war without Parliament's approval. These may or may not succeed. We have to keep up the pressure until they do. You can also write easily to your MP through Fax Your MP or by e-mailing, to urge them to support early day motions, private members bills and other means of bringing pressure to bear.

*Ancient olive grove on Crete*

## Chapter 7

# The Root of the Current Crisis: values; a better balance of male and female energies; psychopathic and narcissistic leaders

 ## Leadership values are at the root of the global crisis

*'The greatest challenge of the 21st Century will be to change the value system underlying the global economy so as to make it compatible with the demands of human dignity and ecological sustainability.'*

Fritjof Capra, 2002

**An underlying value** is that moneymaking, profit, share value, market share and size, should always be more highly prized than human needs and rights, democracy and the environment (Capra, F, 2002). The glorification of material consumption wields tremendous power to maintain optimal conditions for the expansion of production – rather than wellbeing. Power, wealth, consumption, decisiveness and aggression are closely linked to our model of what it is to be a successful male.

**We need to look with scepticism at all Government plans** for modernisation, restructuring and reform. Is there too much male testosterone? Would more be achieved with better leadership and greater respect for the people on the ground? Teachers and hospital staff constantly face new bureaucratic targets, reporting and system changes. Have they been properly involved? We have the most complex, costly and expensive railway system in Europe. Would this have happened with better foresight and proper involvement of people with railway knowledge and experience? Passenger numbers are growing to levels not seen since the fifties, when the network was twice the current size. Yet bold strategic investment to expand the system is not being made. Indeed there are rumours of strategic cuts! Are fares rising above the level of inflation, mainly to pay shareholders, banks and top managers? Many railway staff are alienated. Meanwhile billions are available for war and identity cards.

**A large part of male consciousness includes belief in heroic, top down leadership.** It includes the notion that problems can be solved by violence and war, and a conviction of being right, despite what many people think. We have seen all this in the 'war on terror' and war in Iraq. What a change it would be to say sorry, we got this wrong.

*'The noble art of losing face will one day save the human race.'*

Hans Blix

**Business and politics are bedevilled by the unaware competition of leaders.** We all suffer as a result of the male belief system that values power and domination. Domination of nature is at the root of the industrialisation of agriculture and the promotion of GM food.

**We need to redefine what is 'cool.'** Fast driving in noisy, muscular cars, combined with the ethos of being able to down large quantities of alcohol, still fills our hospitals and morgues and destroys the happiness of thousands of families – apart from the huge cost to the taxpayer, NHS, police and ambulance services and the trauma for people working in these services. At the top end, Virgin boss Richard Branson's exploits in a fast plane creating vast pollution, send out the wrong message. Oxford Brookes University's decision to bestow Jeremy Clarkson, TV's macho 'Top Gear' presenter, with an honorary degree led to protests. World road death statistics are horrific. Each year 1.2 million men, women and children around the world lose their lives as a result of road 'accidents'. Road death is the leading cause of death and disability in the under 35s. 18 to 24 year old men are especially at risk (BBC World Service, Health Matters). I avoid the misleading term *'accidents'* advisedly.

**Patriarchy not only harms women** and denies them their proper place but it harms men just as much. Patriarchy is incompatible with democracy too. *Patriarchy has ruled in almost all religious institutions arguably with harmful effects.* Now, women are steadily gaining leadership in many churches.

**Jane Fonda**, in her speech at the *National Women's Leadership Summit* (16 June 2003,Washington, D.C) said:

*'We have to think about the quality of the men who are with us at the table, the culture that is hovering over the table that governs how things are decided and in whose interests. This is not just about glass ceilings or politics as usual. This is about revolution, and I have finally gotten to where I can say that word and know what I mean by it and feel good about it because I see, now, how the future of the earth and everything on it including men and boys depends on this happening. Let me say something about men: obviously, I've had to do a lot of thinking about men, especially the ones who've been important in my life, and what I've come to realise is how damaging patriarchy has been for them. And all them are smart, good men who want to be considered the 'good guys.' But the Male Belief System, that compartmentalised, hierarchical, ejaculatory, andocentric power structure that is Patriarchy, is fatal to the hearts of men, to empathy and relationship*

*Another thing that I've learned is that there is a fundamental contradiction not just between patriarchy and relationship, but between patriarchy and Democracy. Patriarchy masquerades as Democracy, but it's an anathema.*

*Young Jamaican woman*

*How can it be democracy when someone has to always be above someone else, when women, who are a majority, live within a social construct that discriminates against them, keeps them from having their full human rights?*

*But just because Patriarchy has ruled for 10,000 years since the beginning of agriculture, doesn't make it inevitable.*

*Maybe at some earlier stage in human evolution, Patriarchy was what was needed just for the species to survive. But today, there's nothing threatening the human species but humans. We've conquered our predators, we've subdued nature almost to extinction, and there are no more frontiers to conquer or to escape into so as to avoid having to deal with the mess we've left behind. Frontiers have always given capitalism, Patriarchy's economic face, a way to avoid dealing with its shortcomings. Well, we're having to face them now in this post-frontier era and inevitably – especially when we have leaders who suffer from toxic masculinity that leads to war, the conquering of new markets, and the destruction of the earth."*

—————————ooooooOoooooo—————————

 ## Today we need a better balance of male and female energies

### We have much to learn from wise women leaders

Male energies have served in the past and are still needed. Surely though, right now, we are learning that male dominance is not working in our time? The ancient psyche that still dominates leaders' impulses and actions is inappropriate for the interconnected world of the 21st century. These values, linked to our concept of 'manliness', are changing.

Female energy is about life giving, nurturing, relationships, sensitivity, working together, communication and feeling. We need a balance of the two energies.

**Many brave women around the world are fighting injustice** standing up for human rights and you can read their stories on Amnesty International's website.

Recent Nobel Prize winners, Wangari Maathai and Vandana Shiva put sustainability at the heart of their lives.

**Dr Vandana Shiva,** eminent international Indian physicist, ecological campaigner, women's rights activist and writer – is an eloquent, wise and powerful voice.

*In speaking for agricultural workers in India she speaks for us all – if we only see it.*

**She speaks out against 'mono-culture of the mind'** and the destruction of biodiversity, traditional agriculture and livelihood caused by monoculture, global industrial agribusinesses and the poverty, indebtedness and suicides it causes in the name of 'growth.' The biodiversity of the Punjab, the breadbasket of India, has disappeared and been replaced by monocultures of wheat and rice. Diseases and pests have exploded, and with them the use of pesticides. Chemical farming needs massive inputs of water; overuse of water has lead to desertification. In terms of health, or farmers' incomes, the 'green revolution' has not created 'growth', it has created poverty and under-development – and it devalues women. Devaluation of women in agriculture has led to a new violence in the form of female foeticide. Gender discrimination mutates into women's dispensability under 'development' which excludes and devalues women.

**Women can remove hunger, she argues.** Their knowledge system and technologies produce more while using less – the essence of sustainability. The Millennium Development Goals ignore women friendly alternatives. The patriarchal logic of exclusion is not acceptable to women, nor is defining poverty and wealth on the basis of $1 a day. In women's value system, it is unacceptable that in 2005, 500 million should continue to go hungry. Even when wealth production is not counted in dollars, they are providing food and water. An income of $1 a day is meaningless indicator of development if the cost of living is being pushed up to $10 a day with corporate monopolies on seeds and water because of patents and privatisation.

*Lunchtime in Cuba*

She believes in empowering women and argues that women-centred and earth-centred agriculture systems are more productive; that women's role in agriculture needs to be strengthened both to remove hunger and empower women; that development should be redefined from women's perspective to ensure no one goes hungry or thirsty on this planet. This applies as much to Africa as it does to India. (Based on her full account, written on the train from Punjab, after a day spent with 300 women from rural Punjab, gathered for a Public Hearing organised for the National Commission for Women to assess the impact of globalisation on women in agriculture. (BBC World Service Trust, 10 June, 2004). Listen to her BBC Reith Lecture 2000 and read her new book (Shiva, V, 2000).

**Professor Dr Wangari Maathai**, Kenyan ecologist, first African woman to win the Nobel Peace Prize, at the ceremony in Oslo, Norway, December 2004, urged her audience to recognise that protecting the environment and promoting peace and democracy go hand-in-hand. Since founding a women's Green Belt Movement in Kenya in 1977, she has helped protect people's access to forests and natural resources despite Government attempts to privatise public companies. More than 20 million trees have been planted on women's farms, in schools and church grounds. She has avoided many attempts by President Moi to put her in prison. In 1999, she was attacked while planting trees in the Karura Public Forest, Nairobi, during a protest against the capital's green places being built over. She challenged Moi's power by imprisoning herself in the city cathedral. She urged her audience *'to embrace the whole creation in all its diversity, beauty and wonder'* and warned that if the environment was not protected, peace would forever remain endangered. This applies to Western countries as much as her own, she said, and we need to take to our hearts:

*'In Kenya, one reason why less-industrial peoples haven't yet destroyed their plants and wildlife is that the natural way of life is closely entwined in their lives – and that's their culture. And it's knowledge and wisdom that can be passed to the next generation. Your environment shapes you, even as you shape that environment. Your country is a very important aspect of who you are. Culture is a very important aspect of conservation. We need to see ourselves as part of the family of life. The more industrialised societies become, the more detached from their natural environment and the more they eliminate species. Today, we are faced with a challenge that calls for a shift in our thinking, so that humanity stops threatening its life-support system. If we did a better job of managing our resources sustainably, conflicts over them would be reduced. So, protecting the global environment is directly related to securing peace.'*

**Erica Jong**, in an interview, BBC R4 Today, 13-9-2004, speaking of her new book, *Sappho's Leap,* about the Greek love poet, argues that our civilisation may be in peril, like all the others in the past. Unless we change our priorities, our civilisation is in peril and we too will go. The nuclear threat is emerging once again. Religious extremism on both sides of the Atlantic, is dangerous. We are confused. Do we change our world through war or peace? In the clash between West and Islam, we return to old ways of responding to crisis, used by dictators and tyrants to rally support and hold on to power. Like Hitler, Bush has said, *'you are in danger and only I can save you'* and used a 'War on Terror' to rally a shocked nation, instead of providing an intelligent strategy. Jong argues that we are making a hotbed of terrorists and suicide bombers, enlarging what we most fear. Terrorism cannot be crushed with might. We need to see that people without hope have nothing to live for, become suicide bombers. Rather than bomb, we need to address the root causes – poverty, injustice and disenfranchisement – and offer respect and hope for a decent life with meaning.

———————oooooooOooooooo———————

 # Psychopathic and narcissistic leaders

## Psychopaths

Further interesting insights into our leaders are provided by some recent research. Robert Hare, a 71-year-old professor emeritus from the University of British Columbia, renowned in the field of criminal psychology, applied his Psychopathy Checklist to well known CEOs. They scored as 'moderately psychopathic'. Psychopaths are the 1% of the general population not burdened by conscience.

*'Psychopaths have a profound lack of empathy. They use other people callously and remorselessly for their own ends. They seduce victims with a hypnotic charm that masks their true nature as pathological liars, master con artists, and heartless manipulators.'*

**Corporate psychopaths** score high on Factor 1, the *'selfish, callous, and remorseless use of others'* category. This might help explain the Enron and Worldcom scandals. We are vulnerable to often charming people because we do not realise that not everyone is like ourselves.

*'There are certainly more people in the business world who would score high in the psychopathic dimension than in the general population.'*

### Narcissists

Researcher, Michael Maccoby, identifies the narcissistic CEO as a grandiose egotist who is on a mission to help humanity but is often insensitive to real people around him. Narcissists are visionaries who attract followers. It can make them excel as innovators, but they are poor listeners who can be touchy about criticism. *'These people don't have much empathy,'* Maccoby says. But they do have a sense of changing the world, improving the world. They build their view of what the world should be and recruit others to their vision.

**National culture plays its part:** some countries may be more prone to produce leaders who lift profits and stock prices and are charismatic, visionary and tough. Scandals as Enron and WorldCom aren't just aberrations; they represent what can happen when some basic currents in business culture turn malignant. Read Corporate Psychopaths, Alan Deutschman's article in FastCompany to which I am indebted.

You will provide your own examples!

———————oooooooOooooooo———————

# The 'Beast Within' again!

**Our genes programmed us for survival in earlier times. Survival in the 21st Century requires something else.** The World Health Organisation Report on violence is shocking – rape, murder, shooting, fighting, sexual assault and emotional abuse. Every minute of every day, someone, somewhere in the world, dies because of violence. Globally, there are approximately 1.6 million deaths due to violence each year. That is around half the number of deaths due to HIV/Aids, roughly equal to deaths due to tuberculosis, and 1.5 times the number of deaths due to malaria.

**Victims are everyone** – children, young people, women, men and the elderly. It tears apart families, friends and neighbourhoods, and does untold damage to societies. Fatalities are only a fraction of the full violence problem. Every day, thousands of people need emergency care. It is estimated that each year between 3.5 and 7.5 million people, aged 15 to 29 receive hospital treatment for a violent injury.

In surveys around world, between 10% and 69% of women reported being physically assaulted by an intimate partner at some point in their lives, with many immediate and long-term consequences. One in four women may experience sexual violence by an intimate partner in her lifetime. In females aged 12 to 45 the frequency of pregnancy as a result of rape is 5-18%. In many countries women still have no property rights. Female genital mutilation is widespread in Africa, the Middle and Far East.

**Women give birth and nurture life.** They bring up children and they mourn their lost sons, daughters and partners. It may take a worldwide coalition of women to stop men waging war and other forms of violence. There is a worldwide alliance of women for peace on the roads (Women for worldwide peace on the roads campaign). Two thirds of women, both in the UK and in Europe, are opposed to further nuclear power (Polly Toynbee, *Guardian* 25-11-2005).

**While the world needs more women in leadership, it will be two hundred years before equality reaches Westminster.** EOC research shows that while women make up nearly half the workforce, only a minority attain senior positions in both public and private sectors. Action must be taken now to remove the barriers to women's success. Women hold only about 10% of senior roles in large companies, the judiciary and police. While 20% of MPs are women, the rate at which they are progressing in politics is slower than in other areas. It will take two hundred years for women to gain equal power in politics, unless the main parties make more effort to redress the balance. EOC chairwoman, Jenny Watson said:

*'Thirty years on from the Sex Discrimination Act, it is time for us to face some stark facts. Women will not make it to the top in significant numbers unless action is taken to remove the barriers that stand in their way, and Britain will continue to miss out on women's skills and talents for another generation.'* (BBC News Website 5-1-2006)

*Breadfruit tree*

## Chapter 8
# Making Sense of Globalisation –
# Seeing the System

*'Yet the form of modernity the West has offered to the rest of the world, has been tied to a capitalist ethos and economics which has brought not only growing gaps in income between the top 20% of the world's wealthy and the bottom 20% (that gap was 30:1 in 1960, 60:1 in 1990, and 76:1 in 1998) but also a worldview which has been militantly materialistic, insisting that institutions or social practices be judged rational, productive and efficient only to the extent that they maximise money and power. Though we've told ourselves we were offering economic well being (which is true, for a section of third world populations), and claimed that would bring democracy and human rights as well, the actual experience of many people is that they are being offered a cultural economic package in which consumption is the highest good, and cannot be constrained for the sake of preserving the world's environment or human values. This is a new religion, as much as we once acknowledged communism to be a religion as well, and the human consequences of this religion are already visible in many Western societies: a collection of individuals who know how to 'look out for number one' but who are emotionally and spiritually illiterate, narcissistic, and have great difficulty in sustaining lasting relationships or building solid families. Human relationships are frequently reduced to 'what's in it for me' and our capacity to respond to nature with awe is replaced by a narrow pragmatism that sees commodities rather than mystery.'*

Rabbi Michael Lerner

**We are part of a living system.** The key thing to understand about living systems is they kick back harshly if not respected. Eventually, this may mean that oppressed people will became disillusioned by notions of non-violence, and kick back, in the words of Malcolm X, by 'whatever means necessary,'

This applies equally to the environment and to all the human beings living on the earth. The current economic and political leadership do not show respect for this living system. We are beginning to pay for it.

*Once you understand the living system, you will see it every day.*

**Leaders who do not understand living systems are a danger.** Many deaths in the world occur because we do not see the living system. Tony Blair took us into an unpredictable and disastrous war. Does he see the irony in the West's conflict with Iranian President, Mahmoud Ahmadinejad, over nuclear power and weapons?

**There is growing disillusionment throughout the world,** including USA, with of free trade doctrines and liberal market economics. George Bush went into the 34-nation Latin American Summit on proposed Free Trade Area of the Americas (FTAA), intent on promoting traditional US doctrines, with the goal of a giant free trade area that would stretch from Alaska to the Southern Ocean. He often uses the word 'America' as if *USA* and *America* were the same.

Some 10,000 demonstrators marched through the resort city of Mar del Plata, Argentina, chanting *'Get Out Bush,'* in protest not only at the free trade proposals but at the Iraq war and other US policies. *'We don't have any confidence in anything Mr Bush might propose here,'* said Juan Gonzales, an Argentine trade union leader. Whatever emerged, it *'will only prolong hunger, poverty and death in Latin America,'* he said. The Summit ended inconclusively.

Twenty-nine countries wanted to resume talks on a Free Trade Area of the Americas (FTAA) in 2006. Five others, Brazil, Venezuela, Uruguay, Paraguay and Argentina, whose economy collapsed beneath a mountain of deficits and debt after adopting US and IMF-backed free market policies in the 1990s, insisted on waiting for the results of the WTO meeting in Hong Kong, December 2005. Venezuela's President Hugo Chavez, said they were *'standing like a rock'* against the idea of the free trade area.

**Here is how I see the interconnected system.** Key underlying aspects are lack of respect for the living system including racism. But money plays a most important part.

*'You may find the following helpful in understanding the system of money itself AND of the part it plays in human life and our impact on the planet.*
*The money system is systemic in two respects.*

1. ***Internal.*** *The various elements in the present money system (taxes, public spending, money creation, etc), at national and international level, interconnect and reinforce each others' perverse outcomes; and the necessary reforms and developments based on fairly sharing the value of common resources (tax shift, monetary reform, public expenditure shift – towards people and families and away from business subsidies and contracts – and comparable new developments at international level) will be interconnected elements in a restructured system that produces much more benign and sustainable outcomes.*

2. ***External.*** *The money system as a whole has systemic effects on almost every feature of the larger system of human life and its impact on the planet, because what it rewards and penalises affects almost everything we are able to do and choose to do. These effects are now almost universally perverse.'*

James Robertson

---

**The System**

- Lack of an adequate basic income

- The debt-money system

- Unsustainable taxation

- Tax evasion and money laundering

- The focus on making money rather than meeting human needs

- The myth of GDP and economic growth as a measure of progress

- The instability and power of financial markets

- Stock exchanges wield tremendous power

- Company ownership and company law

- Unrepresentative global institutions

- Racism and lack of respect for difference are at the root

In more detail, this is how it works:

## ● An adequate basic income as of right

It is scandalous that in the UK, 4th wealthiest country, there is so much poverty, especially amongst women and children, and elders who have worked hard in or outside the home. Innumerable proposals over the years have failed to grasp what is both needed and cheapest when everything is taken into account – simple state provision – another example of avoidance and clever, complicating minds.

## ● The debt-money system

Almost all the money we use (except the 3% which is notes and coins) is created, not by central banks and government, but by commercial banks, who charge interest. USA, UK, EU, poor countries and people generally are hugely indebted and burdened with repayments and interest, which increases the cost of everything: prices, investment in health, education, and infrastructure – and the taxes we pay!

> *'... a method so simple the mind is repelled.'*
>
> JK Galbraith

**It's a great way to make money.** In 2006, Barclays unveiled annual profits of £5.28 billion – its share of the £34 billion profits expected from the UK's biggest banks. Global bank HSBC led the field, posting a figure of around £11.5 billion. The second biggest earner was Royal Bank of Scotland, with a figure of around £8.2 billion. Banks make enormous profits whatever goes on in business. It began in Renaissance Italy, making money for bankers and funding trade. We see the results today in Florence's beautiful churches, palaces and art. Later, slavery, colonies, empire, the 'triangular trade' – ships took slaves from Africa to America and the Caribbean; produce from plantations come back to British ports; arms and other manufactures went out from Britain to Africa – all funded by banks. It was a brilliant eighteenth century system for creating wealth. Hawkins and Drake, originally pirates, made fortunes in the triangular slave trade. It funded Britain's industrial leadership in the 18th and 19th centuries. We see the results in our heritage of Georgian country houses, fine cities and art galleries.

**Today we are all enormously indebted:** people, organisations, governments and especially poor countries.

**Arguably, everything costs more as a result** – the system is inflationary and we are storing up problems for future generations.

The need to repay these sums and pay the interest drives unsustainable economic development, causes stress and, anguish, especially when things go wrong.

**The Bank of England estimates consumers now owe £1,004,290,000,000**

(others estimate £1,130,000,000), more than £1,000bn on cards, mortgages and loans. Some 80% of UK personal debt is in the form of loans secured against homes, such as mortgages and re-mortgages. Debt charities warn consumers to think hard about how to manage their debts, if interest rates rise. 66,000 people are predicted to go bust this year. Average household debt is £7,650 (exc. mortgage). Two-thirds of EU credit card debt is British. One in five students owes at least £15,000. Student bankruptcy is a major phenomenon with 4,000 declaring bankruptcy and many more unable to clear their debt. (*Independent on Sunday* 29-1-2006) 40% of women keep debt secret from partners. Half of heavy debtors suffer from depression. (Martin Hickman, Consumer Affairs Correspondent, *Independent*, 03 January 2006)

**Private Partnerships (PPP) and Private Finance Initiative (PFI) may build up a further debt burden for future generations.** The redevelopment of the Royal London Hospital is estimated at £1.89bn making it the most expensive ever NHS PFI, including £479m in fees and interest payments. Network Rail debts are £17bn. Six months' interest payments amounted to £466m (*Guardian* 25-11-05). The Channel Tunnel, providing a more sustainable form of travel than air, grapples with £6.3bn debt. Gordon Brown's proposals, for aid and debt relief to poor countries, would be funded by banks, creating more debt and more profits for banks.

**The need to earn enough to repay large amounts of interest and debt** drives continuous, economic growth and development and bigger and bigger organisations. It puts pressure on companies to grow and earn to cover the debt, and on small businesses and individuals to earn more for the consumer life style it creates. It fuels un-sustainability, as Muslim thinkers argue, because debt-money creates pressure for continuous economic growth. The burden harms poor developing countries especially. It impoverishes us all in the broadest sense – not just the money cost but the pressure and distortion of life style. It is as if we are all 'slaves' to the banks.

**The old idea that usury is a sin finds its place for a second time.** Abe Lincoln – and many of his predecessors were against 'usury.' He printed 'greenbacks' to pay for the Civil War. Still maintained in Islam today, this view was once shared by Christians and Islam alike. The new Pope and a Philippines RC Bishop spoke recently of the immense damage caused by interest. The New Economics Foundation and the Christian Council for Monetary Justice are arguing for fundamental monetary and taxation reform and that money is a public asset to be regulated by government.

● **Unsustainable taxation**
**Currently, taxation is unfair and unsustainable.** It does not sufficiently favour people who make positive contributions to society; it fails to penalise value subtracted such as over-use of natural resources and pollution; it taxes work and enterprise; and it does not sufficiently penalise the

unsustainable or reward and encourage the sustainable. Many subsidies are perverse. The present tax system makes it easier for rich people to avoid tax and poor people pay a higher proportion of their earnings than rich. (Robertson, J, 2003, *Tax Justice Network*)

**The current UK tax system is excessively complicated.** Government makes a diversionary drama of tinkering at the edges, every year making it more complicated. A simpler approach is needed, taxing for the benefit of society: fairer to ordinary people, encouraging the sustainable, taxing the unsustainable, levelling up the costs of products to reflect externalised costs the citizen pays, taxing use of non-renewable resources and actions that harm the environment. This is supported by the Green Alliance and the Policy Studies Institute's latest proposals.

**Gordon Brown's ingeniously complicated and tinkering budget,** presented in an atmosphere of pugilistic point scoring is astonishing given the urgency of the problems the world faces. His measures to discourage the purchase of new gas-guzzling vehicles are unlikely to deter the kind of people who buy and use them. Far bolder action is needed.

**We need a radical overhaul of the tax system** including inefficiency charges on products that waste energy and water and new fiscal incentives to reward consumers for making greener choices. Measures to reduce energy consumption will not work unless accompanied by tougher tax measures. Households currently account for 28% of the UK's greenhouse gas emissions, more than half our water consumption and ten per cent of waste (Green Alliance & Policy Studies Institute).

## ● Tax evasion

According to Oxfam, the New Economics Foundation, the Oxford Council on Good Governance (OCGG) and the Christian Council for Monetary Justice, corporate and super rich individual tax evasion and profit laundering is large scale (Oxfam and World Service 3-1-2006).

**Every year, tax on an estimated £20 billion pounds of corporate profit is being evaded,** mostly by companies setting up offshore trusts where they declare their profits, thus fuelling large scale mergers and acquisitions. Many familiar British companies are based offshore, e.g. in British Virgin Islands, which applies a zero rate of corporate tax. Some US companies pay no tax for their profits as they are declared in the Bahamas. Half of world trade passes through tax havens, even though these minor economies account for a mere 3 per cent of global GDP. Some Trans National Corporations record many intra-company transactions through tax havens to avoid tax. Oxfam estimates assets held offshore, either tax-free or subject to minimal tax, at **Euro 9.2 trillion; over one-third of global GDP**. In the past thirty years, the number of offshore finance centres and tax havens has more than doubled to approximately 60.

**The offshore economy is a key aspect of global capitalism.** The rich get richer partly by evading their minimal citizen duties of paying their taxes. 'Western' states suffer from non-payment of tax; developing countries suffer the worst. Multinationals especially, launder their profits outside their territories, through bogus leasing arrangements to holding companies in the Channel Islands. The same Channel Island bankers and lawyers help ruling elites in developing countries set up offshore accounts in full secrecy for the bribes that multinationals pay to the developing country bureaucrats and dictators.

**Oxfam examines tax havens in relation to developing countries.** At a conservative estimate, tax havens contribute to revenue losses for developing countries of at least US$50 billion a year, roughly equivalent to annual aid to developing countries. Instead of regarding developing countries as unproductive and un-innovative in managing their economies, it is more accurate to say globalisation obliges them to transfer funds on a large scale to 'Western' governments, shareholders and banks, much of this through offshore accounts. Offshore interfaces are the technical side of financial globalisation, along with financial market deregulation and bank created credit. The process is a central feature of what some call **'global monetocracy.'**

## ● Money laundering

Oxfam reveals that a £1trillion business funds terrorism and is used by corrupt politicians. Money laundering and corruption are among the most complex crimes facing the police internationally. Money crimes are very sophisticated and likely to grow with increasing use of IT. It is now possible to transfer funds across the world on the press of a button.

**Private tax evasion and corporate profit laundering** are diminishing the revenues states have to run good public services. The non-payment of tax has led to governments shifting the collection of tax away from businesses. As tax rates for business have decreased in the past 30 years, it is argued, the gaps have been filled by consumption taxes and private income taxes that fall on poorer people disproportionately.

*It would be a great benefit if all offshore financial centres where crime, terrorism, drugs, and western multinationals launder their profits were closed down.*

## ● The focus is on making money rather than meeting human needs

Given the current global financial system, there is little alternative. Until sustainable sources of energy become a major money maker, the emphasis remains on oil exploration and foreign policies and wars to secure oil supplies. The same dynamic applies to food, drink, transportation etc. One of the fathers of gene technology, Nobel prize winner, Professor Sydney Brenner, urges government to spend less on genetically-tailored medicines – and more on public health education, arguing genetic drugs research simply puts profits into the hands of pharmaceutical firms. Public health education could save more lives at less cost. (BBC Radio 4 News, 2-9-2003)

*Financial motives have overtaken the productive purposes of business.*

Sums available for the welfare of ordinary citizens, employees, retired employees and pensioners; needs of developing countries, disadvantaged communities, NHS health trusts, schools and policing are dwarfed by the figures above.

- **'The Myth of Gross Domestic Product' as a measure of progress**

Gross Domestic Product (GDP), dominating national policy, is not an adequate measure of progress. If the primary aim were to meet human needs in a sustainable way and provide work, would growth be needed on such a scale? This requires serious consideration. The 'Western' consumer society, glorifying material consumption, turns us into obsessive workers and consumers. There are other measures like the New Economics

Foundation's Index of Sustainable Economic Welfare (ISEW). According to their paper, *Chasing Progress – Beyond Measuring Economic Growth,* GDP has soared in recent years but a Measure of Domestic Progress (MDR) fell in the seventies and has not recovered. Social Well Being (SWB) has not changed. Meanwhile social and environmental costs such as climate change and resource depletion have risen steadily. A major source of ill health and unhappiness is joblessness and relative poverty. Various studies show there is little correlation between the richest and happiest countries. A Cuban said to me,

*Cuban mountain scene*

*'We are a poor but happy people.'*

**This debate is not the priority it should be.** Governments of advanced countries would better pursue reduction of joblessness, greater social equality and sustainability, rather than economic growth. How to pursue these goals is the interesting issue. We need to get this into our minds – politicians and citizens alike. We have been brain washed!

## ● The instability and power of financial markets

This is a major problem. £2 trillion per day cross the world's computer screens, only 3% of which has anything to do with world trade. This is a major cause of instability. There are proposals for taxing and regulating the huge earnings from these movements (Tobin tax).

## ● Stock exchanges wield tremendous power

Investment analysts exert strong pressure to perform in terms of profits and share value. CEOs may feel under pressure to focus on short-term returns, rather than investing in the long-term, or risk being fired or their companies taken over. The pressure to 'perform' leads to attempts to dominate the market. Mergers and larger and larger organisations result. There is no clear evidence that larger organisations perform better generally, are more efficient in meeting customer needs or better places to work in. Good companies, taken over by foreign owners, may be less committed to local communities. Later they are often closed or moved to another country. This results in anguish for employees, especially if pension obligations are not met. Pressure on competitive performance, together with lower returns on equities, is a factor in the closure of final salary pension schemes. Market pressures contribute to stressful, unsustainable working culture at all levels, contributing to half UK marriages ending in divorce.

## ● Company ownership and company law

Company ownership and financing ties businesses to the short-term pressures and unpredictability of the stock market. A plc is constantly exposed to threat of take-over, instead of enabling it to focus on sustainability, meeting human needs, long term development, serving customers (providing good value), and employees and the community. The current perceived primary duty of directors is to shareholders, to maximise profit and share value, rather than benefiting all stakeholders – society as a whole, the environment, local community, consumers and employees.

> *'Corporations have globalised – but the rules haven't'*
> Barry Coates, Director Oxfam New Zealand

## ● Unrepresentative global institutions

... such as the World Bank, the World Trade Organisation and the International Monetary Fund (IMF), are dominated by the agenda of large corporations and rich nations. They have imposed unfair trading rules, 'structural adjustment programmes', privatisation and a huge burden of debt and interest payments on Third World countries. Theories of undiluted global capitalism, *'free trade'* (not fully applied to our own economies) and *'trickle down'* wealth creation have not worked. We have dumped subsidised goods and destroyed local producers. Commonwealth leaders at their summit in Malta, November 2005, urged the rich developed countries to:

*'... demonstrate the political courage and will to give more than they receive ... particularly in the negotiations on agriculture and market access, as their own longer term prosperity and security depends on such an approach.'*

Underlying this system are two deeper factors: racism and lack of respect for difference, leadership values and the masculine/feminine imbalance described in the previous chapter.

## Racism and lack of respect for difference

Underneath it all, racism and lack of respect for difference is at the root of social injustice, violence and attacks on other countries. This enables *us* to justify exploitation and mistreatment of *others* who are different, like black people, Arabs and Muslims. It manifests in foreign policy and the way we value some lives more than others. Are races different from us somehow – *'unpeople'* to varying degrees?

*Lack of respect for difference is paralleled by our difficulties with people who express contrary views by our not understanding the importance of ecological diversity.*

People realise the system is not working; they are suffering from underlying values that prize moneymaking, profit, share value, market share and size, more highly than human needs, rights and dignity, democracy and the environment (Capra, 2002).

**We need to listen** to wise women like Vandana Shiva (her powerful BBC Reith lecture is still available) and men like Satish Kumar (Resurgence).

The next chapter offers an agenda to address the need for systemic change.

*A park in Seville and a hotel in the Pyrenees*

## Chapter 9

# A New Agenda for the 21st Century

The situation we face is far too serious and urgent to be left to politicians. A sustainable world requires imagination, vision and bold, strategic action. Political process is short term, adverarial and politically expedient.

> *'A first step ... is to seek A New Bottom Line, so that we judge institutions productive, efficient and rational not only to the extent that they maximise wealth and power but also to the extent that they maximise our capacities to be caring, ecologically aware, ethically and spiritually sensitive, and capable of responding to the universe with awe, wonder and radical amazement at the grandeur of creation.'*
>
> Tikkun Community, *A New Bottom Line*

**This chapter is about creating *'capitalism as if the world matters'*** as Jonathan Porritt (echoing Ernst Schumacher's *'Economics As If people Mattered'*, 1973) called it in a recent essay in the *Independent*. Because of its power to change the World, business needs to take a much higher level of responsibility in the 21st century and be proactive, rather than defensive, putting human needs at the top of their agenda.

*It means a shift from sustainability from within existing system limits to a more radical approach of also changing the system.*

**It's time for 'far out' ideas.** We may be at a turning point. People all over the world, know and experience the destructive aspects of globalisation. It is becoming clear: sending aid and 'fixes' are not enough. Fundamental change is needed. We need to address the system.

**It means taking on the challenge of changing the system whilst working in it.** This is what we all have to do every day. Leaders need to give up denial and defensive lobbying and become activists for systemic change. One UK leader who takes action on the big global issues is Anita Roddick. All of them need to take responsibility.

**Here is an agenda for leaders** – i.e. all of us – for action in our work, companies, communities, the way they and we live and campaign for change:

---

# A new agenda
## Challenging the system

✓ Challenge the system.
✓ Promote understanding of the big picture, the urgency of the situation and a new consciousness.
✓ Help people see that values, sexism, racism and lack of respect for diversity, including for nature, are at the root.
✓ Promote measures of progress that reflect well-being rather than GDP.
✓ Democratise global institutions.
✓ Create a new charter framework for licensing large corporations, requiring them to be granted a license to operate.
✓ Reform the debt money system.
✓ Provide a basic citizens' income and citizens' pensions.
✓ Create sustainable and fair taxation.
✓ Regulate financial markets and implement measures such as the Tobin tax.
✓ CSR needs to include companies paying taxes they should pay and accountable accounting systems.
✓ Close tax havens.
✓ Create a new framework for the duties of company directors.
✓ Create fresh legal frameworks for company ownership and financing.
✓ Elevate the importance of sustainable investment.

---

# The new agenda

✓ **Challenge the system** – promote understanding of the big picture and the urgency of the situation, the ways in which the global system is not working; the damage it is causing; and the real cost and threat to human society and the planet.

✓ **Promote a new consciousness** by increasing awareness of the need for a change of values. Instead of putting money first, we need our top priorities to be *public interest, sustainability, meeting human needs* and *giving every human being the chance of a healthy and fulfilling life.*

✓ **Help people see** that values, sexism, racism and lack of respect are at the root of dominating nature, economic exploitation, current foreign policies and those of the dominant global institutions. Deep down, some lives matter less than others.

✓ **Promote measures of progress** that reflect human well-being rather than growth in GDP.

✓ **Democratise global institutions**, like the World Trade Organisation (WTO), World Bank and IMF. Focus on fair, not free trade, and the promotion of human welfare. This means giving something up, actually changing our way of life – being materially poorer but spiritually richer.

✓ **Create a new charter for licensing large corporations**, requiring them to be granted a license to operate. They would be required to justify each year a continued license to operate based on their record of acting with responsibility.

✓ **Reform the debt money system.** We need to look afresh at the debt-money system. This may seem radical 'far out.' It is not the economics taught in school and university. Change would need to be gradual. Many vested interests – almost all of us – are involved. A start could be made with alternative ways of providing low or zero interest money for sustainable environmental projects, economic development in all poor developing countries, where debt is crippling infrastructure, public services, education, health and small businesses. In a democratic age, money should be created as part of a national or supranational money supply by independent monetary authorities such as a National or Regional Banks; international currency by an International Bank. James Robertson and others mentioned have put forward comprehensive proposals (Robertson, J, 2003).

✓ **Provide a basic citizens' income and citizens' pensions.**

> *'The first call on a nation's wealth should be a citizens' income or universal basic income.'*
>
> Peter Challen

**This would offer immense relief to many ordinary people** and the benefits to society would be enormous – less alienation in deprived areas, huge savings in social and health costs resulting from deprivation, in bureaucracy and endless debate about how to end exclusion and create a safer society. Full details are in the books referred to in the previous chapter under the debt-money system.

✓ **Reform taxation** and dismantle corporate and super rich tax avoidance through international agreement; make this an integral part of good governance. The issues are described in the previous chapter. Tax reform needs to be linked to a basic citizens' income and retirement income.

✓ **CSR needs to include paying the taxes the company should pay** under the law and creating accountable accounting systems. Declaring in the CSR statement that this company will refrain from using offshore financial vehicles etc would be a bold step. The Co-operative Bank has done so.

✓ **Close tax havens**, through which half of global trade flows; expose and outlaw the massive profit laundering of corporations, money laundering of criminal and terrorist leagues; tax evasion which is depriving states of their capacity to provide health and education for citizens.

✓ **Create new legal duties for company directors** including strengthening the powers of non-executive board members to monitor sustainable and ethical performance and call directors to account.

✓ **Create fresh legal frameworks for company ownership and financing.** Legislation is needed to facilitate alternatives to the traditional joint stock company. John Lewis Partnership and St Luke's Advertising are examples. In USA, ESOPs (Employee Share Ownership Plans) go far beyond the Anglo-Saxon model of shareholder ownership through the stock exchange. ESOPs cover more than 9 million workers in more than 10,000 firms. (Job Ownership)

✓ **Investment analysts need to elevate the importance sustainable investment.** There are encouraging initiatives with many stock exchanges; progress is made but there is along way to go in making sustainable investment a priority in the minds of analysts and financial advisors. They need to be proactive in helping their increasingly aware clients.

✓ **Regulate financial markets** and implement measures such as the Tobin tax. The Tobin Tax (see Resources or google) proposes a simple sales tax on currency trades across borders which would discourage short-term currency trades – about 90 percent are speculative – but leave long-term productive investments intact.

(For comprehensive ideas about money, debt, taxation and citizens' incomes and pensions including taxing the value of common resources which derive from Nature, like unextracted energy, or land values enhanced by the activities of society as a whole such as public developments, see Robertson, J, 2003 and Resources and References)

**Many of these ideas are radical. Mindful change is needed.** The best way is to create awareness of the need for change and the possibilities. Then creativity will come into play.

We'd have to be prepared to give something up. The way is to proceed step by step, starting with small changes, those that would make the biggest difference. We'd have to create common ground and not focus where there is major disagreement.

> *'Problems cannot be solved at the same level of consciousness that created them.'*
>
> Albert Einstein

*Restaurante Modesto in Seville*

**A New Consciousness is Emerging.** Information leads to greater awareness. With awareness comes a change in consciousness. Many people realise everyone needs to be a world citizen if human beings are to enjoy a secure and sustainable future. Maybe we are at a turning point.

> *'Nothing changes without personal transformation.'*
>
> Dr WE Deming

As we get older or mature, we move from focusing on 'me' to 'us' to 'all of us.' A similar process may take place in global society. Ken Wilber and Don Beck believe individual human beings and societies are at different stages of consciousness and the trend is upward. They estimate some 50 million adults in the United States and probably about 80-90 million in the European Union have worldview values.

> *'Is the new American dream really about getting and spending, and being the first zillionaire on the block?*
>
> (Cultural Creatives)

*A diverse group of people working with Bruce*

## *Chapter10*
# How to Change Things for the Better – for Everyone

No one really knows how to do this. We continue to explore how to do it. We seem to learn more with every success and failure. Our historical memories are short and each generation re-learns to do it in their own way but the new media helps our memories.

---

**EXAMPLE 1:**

**RIGHT WAY – A benign example of how to change things for the better,** is the new Evelina Children's Hospital, completed 31st October 2005, the first new hospital for children to be built in London in over one hundred years.

*It was designed by children for children. Hopkins Architects worked with a board of consultants ranging in age from five to fifteen, and consequently the lifts look like rockets, x-rays take place in the arctic, patients sleep in the mountain or on the beach, and a giant swirly slide dominates the waiting room. BBC's Jennifer Chevalier visited it and discovered a good environment can help children and their parents get better faster and helps staff flourish and love to come to work.* (Thanks to BBC's Jennifer Chevalier, BBCNews.co.uk)

---

---

**EXAMPLE 2:**

**WRONG WAY – Bring New Orleans Back**. It looks as if despite good intentions, they did not spend enough time involving citizens at the outset. The BNOB commission spent three months assessing the city's future. Set up by Mayor Ray Nagin, it proposed to rebuild the city, devastated by Hurricane Katrina, and restore it to its former glory. Possibly the costliest rebuilding programme in US history, when made public, a group of New Orleans residents expressed anger at the recommended four-month moratorium on rebuilding homes in some affected districts. Mr Nagin said flood-ravaged residents would have to face 'harsh realities.'

His report was *'controversial'* and *'pushes the edge of the envelope.'* Anger erupted against developer Joseph Canizaro: *'I don't know you, but Mr Canizaro, I hate you,'* said one resident *'You've been in the background scheming to take our land.'* *'Our neighbourhood is ready to come home,'* and another, *'Don't get in our way and prevent us from doing that. Help us cut the red tape.'* The full report, eventually to be presented to federal government – may include a 53-mile light railway system, new jazz district, as well as recommendations on how to prevent future flooding. (Based on contemporary news reports on websites.)

---

**Our world calls for a new mindset.** The talk of politicians and top business people, *'driving change; delivering change'* and *'putting in place'* (as if this were possible!) is misleading. By now, there is enough evidence that it is more complex than that. We do not have this kind of control and it is foolish to pretend! These awful mechanistic phrases – without respect for human dignity – contribute to the way most big organisations deplete the human spirit and wear people out. It is why so many well-intentioned changes disappoint and have to be reversed a few years later. Good people get out – they do not want to be treated like cogs in a machine.

**The 21st Century needs a fresh understanding of how to create communities and workplaces fit for people** – how to bring about change, how to lead and how to reach forward in ways that benefit everyone.

**When change initiatives fail** to achieve the hoped for outcomes, it is often because they are top-down changes; people closest to the situation or most affected (e.g. businesses, education, health, railways, police, local government) were not involved enough. Change fails when imposed without an understanding of the needs of the human spirit or respect for people's rich knowledge and creativity.

*'In our experience, enormous struggles with implementation are created every time we deliver changes to the organisation rather than figuring out how to involve people in their creation.'*

Wheatley, M and Kellner-Rogers, M, 1998

*'In reality, people do not resist change; they resist having change imposed on them.'*

Capra, F, 2002

Also, it is important to remember that both *restraining* and *crusading* forces need to be respected (Polarity Management). So often the former are seen as an annoying obstacle, rather than a gift from people who care deeply but may be afraid to speak their minds plainly.

—————————oooooooOooooooo—————————

## Emerging thinking about change

We need to embrace new thinking about how change takes place. The essence of this is that organisations are complex, self-regulating, open, living systems, apparently disorderly but actually, like nature, an orderly chaos. Chaos, as a stage in the process of change, is to be embraced rather than feared, controlled or avoided. We have to be brave enough to face chaos. We cannot rely on command and control. Like the whole of life, organisations and people will not be controlled. The same applies in our closest relationships.

Meg Wheatley and Fritjof Capra learned by studying nature.

*'You can't impose change on anything alive. It will always react; it will never obey. This is one of the principles I've embraced for years. ... We look at all that and we say they are resisting change, but they're not. They are responding like all life does – they are reacting.'*
Meg Wheatley, 2002, *The Servant Leader - From Hero to Host*

*'The main contrast is between the metaphor of organisations as machines and that of organisations as living systems'*
Fritjof Capra, 2002

*Mangrove swamp in Jamaica - an important part of the eco-system*

> ## Emerging thinking about organisations
> *Dealing with the unknown, we face unprecedented speed of change, complexity, uncertainty, ambiguity and unpredictability ...*
>
> - everything is interconnected
> - organisations are open, self-organising living systems
> - not machines but living systems like nature
> - chaos is to be embraced as part of transformation, creation
> - recognition that we are not in control
>
> *So ...*
>
> - ways forward emerge, often out of chaos
> - importance of purpose, values, relationships and process in guiding us through complexity and chaos
> - skills needed: synchronicity, non-linear thinking, intuition, spirit, paradox, dialogue, polarity management, left and right brain, yin and yang, whole system, whole person, both personal and global sustainability.

If we are to make wise decisions and lead well in this chaotic, complex, transforming world, we need to accept **the importance of uniting body, mind, heart and spirit.** People want greater meaning and balance.

> *'There is an Indian proverb or axiom that says that everyone is in a house with four rooms, a physical, a mental, an emotional and a spiritual. Most of us tend to live in one room most of the time but, unless we go into every room every day, even if only to keep it aired, we are not a complete person.'*
> Godden, R, (1990) *A House with Four Rooms*

**If we achieve that balance, we are more likely to succeed** in creating successful, sustainable organisations and a fairer and sustainable world. We may also attract good people to our organisations and engage their passion and creativity. Work needs to be holistic – integrating mind, heart, spirit and body. Energy and spirit are needed for creativity. We can't be creative and full of good energy when we are depleted and burnt out. This means giving ourselves time for reflection, and offering processes like meditation, Tai Chi, Yoga, Qigong, as part of workplace culture.

**We need to look at how organisations actually change.** Organisations are self-organising, living systems. They change and adapt through informal social networks, as much as through formal structures. We need both formal and informal.

*'The aliveness of an organisation – its flexibility, creative potential and learning capability – resides in its informal communities, ... networks – alliances and friendships ... channels of communication ... and other tangled webs of relationships – that continually grow, change and adapt to new situations.'*

Capra, F, 2002

Organisations were always like this but it is especially relevant today.

———————————oooooooOooooooo———————————

**So, what are the implications** for top people or anyone, like you or me, who wants to lead well? The world is in great need of wise leadership.

**At the beginning of the 21st century we need a more complex approach to leadership.** Leaders need to learn: what worked in the past may not work now; a more complex approach is needed than got us by in the past – not so much the heroic approach but a more enabling one.

Leaders now need to do two things well:

✓ on the one hand, offer an appealing message about purpose, values, vision, direction and culture

✓ on the other, enable the organisation to respond, adapt, co-create, re-create and replace itself as a living system.

There are two ways of creating the future: there are **designed futures**, which are first created in our imagination; secondly, **emergent futures** (Capra, F, 2002). The essence of the new leader's role is enabling and challenging.

---

### 21st Century leadership - the duality of leadership

21st Century leaders need to do two things exceptionally well: *inspire* and *enable*.

Two ways of creating the future:
- *designed future*, first created in our imagination
- *emergent future*.

And:
- *making things happen* ... and
- *letting go and allowing things to happen*.

Leaders need both *charisma* and the *wisdom to be enabling servants*.

---

**It is so frightening we can hardly face it** – as well as exciting and full of promise. We are in the midst of global transformation. People everywhere face unprecedented uncertainty about the future: global competition; the threat of massive and unpredictable climate change; international terrorism. China, India, Latin America – the new powers – and Islam are emerging as powerful forces. To respond well, we need to allow ourselves to feel and be aware!

## Relationships are vital

*'The only way to lead when you don't have control is you lead through the power of your relationships. You can deal with the unknown only if you have enormous levels of trust, and if you're working together and bringing out the best in people. … It is possible to prepare for the future without knowing what it will be.'*

Meg Wheatley, 2002
*The Servant Leader – From Hero to Host*

————————ooooooOoooooo————————

**Workplaces need a cultural revolution.** To thrive and survive, organisations need to continuously innovate, offer excellence – or die. As the Japanese model has shown, that is not possible without the collective intelligence of the whole organisation. No one person, however able, can possibly know what needs to be done. We need to co-create – releasing everyone's initiative, enterprise and creativity.

**'Getting the whole system into the room.'** We are more likely to find wise ways forward with our complex issues, whether in organisations or in our global society, if we 'get the whole system into the room' and work as whole people – uniting mind, heart, body and spirit. In that way, there will be more hope for the future. This means using process structures for strategic decision making that involve all stakeholders. (Marvin Weisbord and Sandra Janoff, 1995)

————————ooooooOoooooo————————

**Servant leadership.** Business leaders are more than ever aware of the need for corporate citizenship. There is also growing awareness of the need for servant leadership. Servant leadership is a very old idea, expressed in many faiths. Servant leaders understand the importance of creating a culture that releases human spirit. One of the best exponents of servant leadership is Meg Wheatley. In the UK, John Noble heads the **Robert Greenleaf Centre for Servant-Leadership UK**.

**Robert Greenleaf** gave what many consider the best description of the servant-leader:

*The servant-leader is servant first. It begins with the natural feeling that one wants to serve, to serve first. Then conscious choice brings one to aspire to lead.*

*The difference manifests itself in the care taken by the servant-first to make sure that other people's highest priorities are being served. The best test, and difficult to administer, is: Do those served grow as persons? Do they, while being served, become healthier, wiser, freer, more autonomous, more likely themselves to become servants? And what is the effect on the least privileged in society; will they benefit or, at least, not be further deprived?*

Here's my version.

---

# Leading change wisely

**Servant leaders:**

✓ keep world citizenship, sustainability and global social justice top of the agenda

✓ are leaders of leaders

✓ practice respect for diversity

✓ practice personal and corporate responsibility

✓ get the whole system, all stakeholders, into the room and encourage the full diversity of views

✓ make it safe for people to be who they are and express their truth

✓ encourage the belief that we learn by making mistakes – fear of admitting them or being judged does not help

✓ work towards common ground and 'joined up' change

✓ encourage individual expression of visions of a desirable future for the world, their workplace and themselves, based in values and purpose

✓ see change as a cultural issue – to increase people's capability to transform things for the better and learn continuously

✓ help people embrace change, uncertainty, complexity and chaos as part of transformation and creativity

✓ share control

✓ lead in a way that releases spirit, enables innovation, encourages personal responsibility and allows people to work from joy, passion and energy

✓ model their values and beliefs in their behaviour as much as they can

✓ sustain themselves and encourage others to do the same

✓ support others in fulfilling their highest purpose.

---

**Co-creation.** Instead of imposing strategies without involving people 'on the ground', wasting their knowledge and dedication, leaders need to co-create with their people. Collectively, the people in an organisation best understand the situation. Together, they are the best people to change it. Leaders need to create a culture that liberates the human spirit in their organisations; releases all that unused energy, intelligence and creativity, blocked by society in the past, still blocked by lack of confidence, cynicism and the history of being dis-empowered. Leaders need to encourage people to take responsibility and make it safe for them to enjoy being who they really are.

*'The right way to do things is not to persuade people you're right but to challenge them to think it through for themselves.'*

Noam Chomsky

**The way human beings learn is messy.** A lot happens by bumping into each other and relating. That is why conversations are so important. We are more like termites than we might like to acknowledge. All of us play a part in this process. Things transform whatever we do. It is up to each of us to decide what unique part we want to play in this, where our energy lies, where our passion will take us.

**Very simple processes.** To bring about change successfully, we need processes everyone can relate to and use. The basic essentials are:

---

## Simple processes - to release the human spirit

### Monologue is boring

- **Include all key stakeholders** and the full diversity - 'the whole system in the room'.

- **Sit in a circle** as human beings have done for thousands of years (at our best - we have also slaughtered each other).

- **Share individual hopes** and agree common purpose and desired outcomes.

- **Seek common ground**.

- Start to **identify the most important questions** to address

- **Focus energy** on the desired state, vision.

- **Appreciate what is working**. Study what works and create more of it. Focusing on problems and difficulties does not usually work - **what you focus on enlarges!**

- **See ourselves as partners**, all responsible.

---

- **Work in ways** that reflect how change emerges and develop the skills for that

- **Provide an 'Open Space'.** (Open Space)

- **Create a culture of trust**, where everyone feels accepted for who they are, able to speak their truth and well supported in fulfilling their highest purpose.

- **Celebrate**; enjoy laughter; engage heart, spirit, mind and body.

- Everyone has **equal opportunity** to contribute his or her thinking and people listen to each other with respect and without interruption

- **Agree to non-violent communication.** Treat everyone well and with respect. (NVC)

- **Everyone, as partners, shares responsibility** for outcomes and agrees to honour what they have taken responsibility for.

- **Work in a variety of groupings**: pairs, small groups and the whole group.

- **Be aware of our unconscious tendency to group think, avoid, deny, blame, project onto others and sabotage. Get it out 'into the room'.**

- **Provide time for quiet reflection.**

- **Provide for 'joining up' strategic change** without deadening spirit

- **Plan and make it happen:** a follow-on structure for regularly reviewing and celebrating progress and giving and receiving support.
- **At the end, review the process** - share what worked well; what needs to be different next time; learning.

**Nelson Mandela's statement of principles** (Chapter 13) **is a guiding light**. Enormously challenging to practise, it applies to gatherings of whatever size within organisations, communities and families.

Changing your world or yourself, as you well know, is not easy. Here is what I have learned.

# Simple Wisdom

❇ First, discover who you are, why you are on the planet, find your purpose; work towards being fully who you are.

❇ Dream, trust your dreams and inner messages - follow your heart.

❇ Be a leader of leaders - we are all leaders.

❇ Believe the universe will support you.

❇ Understand you are part of a larger process of transformation.

❇ Live in Rumer Godden's *Four Rooms* each day.

❇ Challenge yourself by listening to diverse views; respect difference and other people's reality.

❇ Face conflict.

❇ Have good friends who support you well in fulfilling your highest purpose.

❇ See difficulties as gifts.

❇ Give yourself whatever nurtures your spirit.

❇ Let go of the old to let in the new.

❇ Remember: chaos is part of transformation.

❇ Intuition works in reflection or sleep and makes sense of complexity and confusion.

❇ Be open to synchronicity.

❇ Don't avoid feelings - feelings heal and are your teacher.

❇ Appreciate others and yourself.

❇ Celebrate.

❇ Know what really matters and be grateful for it.

More about simple processes and global issues can be found in my website *Creating Better Workplaces for the 21st Century* **www.brucenixon.com** and books, *Making a Difference* and *Global Forces*, including the **Strategic Leadership Model,** a reliable flexible structure for many situations.

*Dr Keith Panton with Bruce*

## Chapter 11
# A Visit to Jamaica – Heaven and Hell

*In the Sixties, I worked for Alcan Jamaica. Jamaica was just Independent from the British Empire. It was an exciting, hopeful place. Far-sighted statesman Norman Manley was Premier. He saw the need for federation in the Caribbean. That lost him the next election. His wife and soul mate, Edna, a brilliant artist, influenced by the revolutionary work of William Blake, as a young Slade art student, played a key role in the rebirth of thriving Jamaican art and culture. Her work can be seen in the Jamaica National Gallery. Their son, the late Prime Minister Michael Manley, and others in the family continued and continue this inspiring tradition for a better Jamaica.*

*In November 2004, with Suzanne, my partner, I went back for a third time to give the international keynote talk at the Jamaica Customer Service Association annual conference on the invitation of Ilsa DuVerney. We spent time with her and my former colleague Dr Keith Panton, ex CEO and Chairman of Alcan Jamaica – we met when young men. Being back was inspiring, moving and shocking. Jamaica could be paradise on Earth but the situation has worsened.*

**You have to experience it to understand it** and even then you won't – not from a gated tourist resort or a big cruise ship, but, on the ground if you dare, with street-wise friends who will keep you out of trouble. Most people in US, UK and EU do not realise how fortunate they are and have not experienced the situation so many good people face in countries like Jamaica. We were upset and angry to see it.

**Jamaica is extraordinarily beautiful** – mountains, hills, shores, clear blue sea, an ideal climate (bar hurricanes), fertility, a great variety of vegetables, fruit and fish, beautiful flowering shrubs and trees and superb local food. Jamaicans are generally warm, courteous, exciting, resourceful, brave and talented people.

*Jamaica's Blue Mountains*

**Jamaica is small enough** that you get involved in its national life. To help promote the conference, I did a short interview on a radio programme – *Breakfast Club* – hosted by the talented Beverley Manley, former wife of ex Premier, the late Michael Manley.

I met the new Vice Chancellor of the excellent University of West Indies at its beautiful site below the Blue Mountains. They suffered a 25% budget cut – more to come – and growing competition from new tertiary institutions. Meanwhile, I reflected, billions are spent on the so-called 'war on terror' and 'regime change.' Two national papers, Gleaner and Observer, with excellent articles on the situation in Jamaica and the world, are pillars of democracy.

**Jamaica's colonial Georgian and Nineteenth century architectural heritage,** comparable with Williamsburg in USA, could be a huge attraction.

Tragically, much of it decays for lack of money – not ideas – to restore it. Kingston is still full of lovely architecture and Jamaica's extraordinary history. Upper Kingston, with the University campuses under the spectacular Blue Mountains, is still affluent and beautiful. Once charming and prosperous, old stores in Downtown are declining or gone. The renowned Kingston Botanical Gardens have deteriorated.

**We visited the National Art Gallery in Kingston** where there was a large exhibition of Rasta Everald Brown's extraordinary work, much of Edna Manley's beautiful pieces and a wealth of other Jamaica artists through the years. Though comparable to the best medium-sized galleries in Europe, during our long morning visit there were only three or four other visitors, including a busy school child and two Japanese visitors. Was it fear of crime in downtown Kingston, lack of publicity or something else that kept people away? In any European city, it would be a big attraction and a favourite meeting place.

**Desperate poverty and a very large gap between rich and poor** – 'haves and have nots' – seems worse despite the large amount of development that has taken place. There is money, but wealthy Jamaicans seem reluctant to invest in Jamaica. There are some real 'no go' areas and you could easily step into trouble in side streets. Places like Trench Town (known world-wide through Bob Marley's plangent songs) are distressing – and frightening. Poverty in Downtown Kingston and places like historic Spanish Town is shocking. Violence and crime are a great worry to Jamaicans. Shootings are common – mostly gangs killing each other, not other people, though there are horrifying exceptions. In a country with about 2.7 million people, in the first ten months of 2004, nearly 1,300 had been killed. According to the Economist, on a per capita basis, Jamaica has the highest murder rate in world, ahead of South Africa and Colombia. As visitors we felt insecure, especially after dark, except when minded by friends who spot trouble or someone following their car. Our driver taking us to Norman Manley Airport on the Palisades at Kingston asked us to allow him to get home in daylight and often travelled with a colleague.

**We listened to dozens of Jamaicans** in many different walks of life and levels in society, including Rastafarians. A businessman I talked with, bathing in the Caribbean, believes Bush has been bad for business, causing instability in the world. Others expressed their perception of US greed, arrogance, interference and domination, echoing the British Empire in bygone times. The first thing everyone talks about is violence, crime and the effect it has on attempts to rejuvenate the economy, a vicious downward spiral. Fishermen complain their nets and traps are stolen or raided. Violence, crime and corruption result from an unjust global society and lack of opportunity. They obstruct efforts to bring investment and create enterprises and employment. There is talk of corruption in Government, the police, the civil service and unfairness in the courts. Health and education have deteriorated. Teachers now work two shifts to save money; afternoon children get tired, worn out teachers. Driving back to Kingston, we saw an injured person lying in the road. I was concerned that people moving him off the road would cause further damage. Our driver said there was little chance of getting an ambulance promptly. Along the road, we saw teenage women with babies. They destroy their chances by getting pregnant as a way of gaining financial support – they hope.

Some of these issues affect us in affluent UK. In Jamaica they are extreme and crippling.

*Blue Mountain cabin*

**We stayed in a cabin 4,000 feet up in the Blue Mountains.** The wind blew, the rain lashed down and the clouds wet our clothes overnight, rather like Wales, except when the clouds clear you see a tropical city and the Caribbean below. Caused by two recent hurricanes, landslides intruded on mountain roads and fallen trees blocked trails. So we could not hike. On the way up the winding road, we passed beautiful homes in the mountains and later stopped at a splendid café with superb views. At one point, we were delayed, while a huge boulder from a landslide was pushed off by a group of soldiers.

**Later we stayed in a cottage at Treasure Beach** on the South Coast, hot and dry, not much visited by tourists. Friendly, civil and kindly local people soon look after us and it feels like a community. The South Coast – the agricultural breadbasket of Jamaica – suffered badly from hurricanes. With an enterprising attitude they *'thank God it was not worse and be thankful for our blessings'* and get on with rebuilding their homes, businesses and lives. Most Jamaicans are religious – part of how they cope, by thanking God for their blessings – *'Hurricane Ivan could have been worse.'* It wrecked shops, restaurants, hotels and houses; ruined beaches; moving the sand away in some cases; tore down the coconut palms and in many places stripped the leaves off every tree. There were hardly any local fruit, fruit juices or vegetables at the roadside or in shops. There would not be much fruit that year, though the leaves came back rapidly. Waves 20 – 30 feet high had rushed through houses and the wind took roofs off. The water tank had been blown off our cottage. We had no hot water but the outside shower was warm enough.

*Jamaican family on Treasure Beach*

**Rastas say the 'West' is Babylon** – excessive consumption, greedy lifestyle, creating shortages, polluting the air, seas and land! Seems pretty astute to me! At first I was nervous and stressed. By mistake, I gave Rasta Stanley a J$1,000 note instead of J$100, paying him for a carved button wood paper knife. He asked me to show him my money. He replaced the wrong note and picked out the correct one. I asked him not to tell my wife. I felt silly. He gave me a little lesson.

*'Sir, you need to learn to handle your money,'* and, *'honesty is the best policy.'*

Next day, we met again. Suzanne bought from him a beautiful carved pendant, representing the harmony of male and female. As the sun set over the Caribbean, Rasta Stanley sat down with us by the beach. We had a long, deep talk. A short demonstration of the benefits of Corporate Social Responsibility!

**It is hardly surprising that poor people resort to growing marijuana or working for drug barons** who at least provide employment. What would you do if you were desperate, bombarded with US lifestyle on TV? We complain of local people pestering. Surprising in the circumstances? It is the same here: all those intrusive TV advertisements, paper in letterboxes, callers at the door, telephone and internet intrusions. Consultants like me hustle to get work. What difference? There is plenty of rich people corruption in the 'West'.

**Unemployment is 40 per cent** – according to an unofficial estimate. The national debt burden is scandalous. Interest payments to the International Monetary Fund and other sources, not loan repayments, amount to over 60 per cent of GDP. In one year, Jamaica paid out $17.05 in debt service for every $1 received in aid grants. USA and the European Union, whilst dumping their own heavily subsidised products, impose free trade on countries like this. They also charge heavy import duties on their products. Jamaica struggles to compete against the products of cheaper labour in Asia and Latin America. Of course the lingering aftermath of colonisation and slavery still pervades at a deeper level. But the root of the problem is an unfair trading regime that benefits rich countries at the expense of poor. Structural Adjustment Programmes, requiring privatisation, imposed by the IMF as a condition for loans, have undermined public health and education.

*Suzanne with Jamaican friends*

We were deeply affected by the generosity we experienced and the realisation of how dire things are in Jamaica. Despite their talent, enterprise and inspiring efforts, they really do not stand a chance, given the debt burden and unfair global trading system. It shocked us.

*In the UK, most people have no idea how fortunate or what a small minority we are.*

**We stayed at an affluent hotel.** Inside it was just like the USA, with US people doing what they do, a sort of colony. At first I felt angry. Is ignorance an excuse for what boils down to exploitation and oppression – imperialism in a new form. The complex had destroyed the character of a beautiful area but restored a Great House. Then I realised what opportunities and training it was giving talented Jamaicans. One very intelligent waiter said US people are 'innocent.' Is that too kind?

**Surely it is time to give something back.** When you look at our stately homes and Georgian and Victorian cities in the UK, consider where that wealth came from, and how our banking system and industrial revolution were financed. Jamaica helped make Britain rich. Some of the funds for

Tate Galleries in England came from the profits of Jamaican sugar. Slavery, Empire and Colonies were big ideas for making a lot of money. Banking was another brilliant invention. The latest idea for making a lot of money, at the expense of poor countries, is a combination of imposed free trade, subsidised dumping, structural adjustment, lending and globalisation! I thought again of Bush's *'regime change'*, *'freedom loving peoples'* and *'freedom'* to do what? – new Empire building?

**Trickle down theories of the World Trade Organisation, World Bank and the IMF** are un-researched and unproven – dogmas, driven essentially by Western greed, arrogance, lack of respect and imposition – however unaware or 'innocent,' as our Jamaican waiter said? It is time to listen, respect and give something back – if we really want a more peaceful and secure world. Poverty and unfairness are greater threats than international terrorism. Jamaica was once our major source of bananas. Now, I never see Jamaican fruit and vegetables. Why no Jamaican Traidcraft, Jamaican Fair Trade chocolate or Percol Blue Mountain coffee?

**There can be no peace or peace of mind whilst there is such injustice.** Do we want a just and sustainable World in which every young person has the prospect of a fulfilling, safe and healthy life? Do we want billions spent on wars on terror and regime change or on people?

**I thought about all the grants Andalusia has received** from the European Community: for planting fruit and olive trees, roads, infrastructure, railways, power and water. Just visualise Jamaica if it received grants like that – plus education, health services, hospitals, security. Would Caribbean Regionalisation, perhaps with Latin America, be part of the answer? Perhaps Norman Manley's belief in federation was far ahead of its time.

**What can we do?** Removing enormous obstacles the 'West' has created would help Jamaica find its own solutions. Countries like Jamaica have little chance under the current global trading regime. They cannot compete. Jamaica is not one of the 18 countries within the World Bank's Heavily Indebted Poor Countries initiative debt relief measures agreed at the G8 Summit July 2005 (Jubilee Research). Current EU reforms will bear down heavily on counties like Jamaica.

 *If you feel strongly, lobby your MP and MEP, PM and Ministers, the World Trade Organisation, World Bank, and join the many campaigns for fair trade, cancelling 'Third World' debt and for trade justice. Keep up the pressure on Chancellor Gordon Brown and Prime Minister Tony Blair to fulfil their promises. Find the World Development Movement, Jubilee 2000, Jubilee Research, Oxfam and Christian Aid and support their campaigns. Take a look at what Joseph Stiglitz says about the IMF (Google).*

*Grandpa and Grandma Bartoli*

*Chapter 12*

# Crazy Idealists and Heroes
## – who change the world

## Introduction

The idea of this chapter came to me after visiting the Centre for Alternative Technology (CAT), near Machynlleth in Wales where I picked up a copy of *Crazy Idealists? The CAT Story*. My partner, Suzanne, and I stayed nearby on a tranquil and beautiful small-holding created by two 'crazy idealists' who moved there from Croydon in the seventies and are almost self-sufficient in food. That gave me added inspiration. Today CAT is a thriving and beautiful source of inspiration, full of applications of new technologies and examples of what can be done by people like you and me. It is also a very good source of information about sustainable building processes and materials and every aspect of sustainable living including growing food.

**The Centre for Alternative Technology** is built on the site of a disused slate quarry where the last owner died in an accident. There could hardly have been a less hospitable site when work started on creating it in the seventies. Most of us know what Wales is like in the rain! It was the vision of the founder Gerard Morgan-Grenville, supported by many others including John and Audrey Beaumont, who owned the land. They realised that the vision required a mixture of people – idealists, skilled technical pioneers and pragmatic entrepreneurs – with the determination to see it through from small, unpromising beginnings to the busy, successful place it is today. They faced many obstacles and setbacks, and often extremely tough conditions. One of these people of the early days was Liz Todd who wrote:

*'We used to eat all our meals in the engine shed. We were surrounded by sacks of cement and bags of coal. Mice, voles and little shrews used to run around.'*

**Crazy idealists change the world.** Sometimes I feel discouraged about the size of the problems we face and how difficult it all seems. Then I think about all those crazy idealists and heroes who are changing the world or have done so throughout history, often needing great personal courage.

First, **the brave slaves in Jamaica** who rebelled, often suffering great cruelty and losing their lives, eventually supported by idealists like **William Wilberforce**; then, Crimean war veteran nurse and original lady of the lamp, black **Mary Seacole** whose fame now rivals Florence Nightingale's; **Rosa Parks**, the black seamstress whose refusal to relinquish her seat to a white man on a city bus in Montgomery, Alabama, almost 50 years ago helped touch off the civil rights movement of the 1950s and 1960s. The more I learn about history, the more I realise what a battle it has been.

**Elizabeth David,** in the thirties and forties, had a passion for the good, simple food of Mediterranean countries where people care what they eat. She used garlic, alien to Britons, and during rationing bought olive oil – then classified as medicine – from chemists! Mocked for her ideas, she never gave up. Her beautiful books eventually transformed our taste, preparing the way for the likes of Jamie Oliver. UK sales of 'liquid gold', as Homer called olive oil, have risen 40% in five years to £104m compared with lard, down 35% to £14m a year.

As long ago as 1946, **Lady Mary Balfour**, founded the now enormously influential Soil Association, dedicated to natural and chemical free farming and food production and opposition to GM. Another lonely voice, she foresaw the crisis that exists today.

**Books can powerfully influence social change.** In 1962 **Rachel Carson's** prophetic *Silent Spring*, exposed the hazards of the pesticide DDT and challenged humanity's faith in technological progress. She set the stage for the environmental movement. This courageous woman took on the chemical industry and raised important questions about humankind's impact on nature. In 1973, **Ernst Friedrich Schumacher**, pioneer in ecological studies, alternative technology and sustainable development, published *Small is Beautiful – Economics as if People Mattered*. It was to have an enormous influence and continues to do so. His legacy includes the internationally renowned Schumacher College and Resurgence magazine.

*'Perhaps we cannot raise the winds. But each of us can put up the sail, so that when the wind comes we can catch it.'*

EF Schumacher

**Sir Freddie Laker's** Skytrain 'failed' but paved the way for Virgin and EasyJet.

**Jamie Oliver's** Channel 4 TV programmes started a revolution to get junk food out of schools and have dinner ladies trained to provide nourishing meals for our children. Government had to be pushed hard to make changes. Jamie's credo is:

*'The only plan I've got is to try to do everything from the heart.'*

**Italy's Slow Food campaign** was started in 1986 by Carlo Petrini, provoked by the incursion of American-style fast food chains, and is comparable to **Joseph Bove's non-violent civil disobedient 'Confederation Paysan.'** Both continue to inspire worldwide movements. Petrini's manifesto bewailed the fact that:

*'We are enslaved by speed and have all succumbed to the same insidious virus, Fast Life, which ... forces us to eat Fast Foods, which diminish opportunities for conversation, communion, quiet reflection and sensuous pleasure, thus short-changing the hungers of the soul. In the name of productivity, Fast Life has changed our way of being and threatens our environment and our landscapes. Our defence should begin at the table with Slow Food. Let us rediscover the flavours and savours of regional cooking.'*

*The Bartoli Agriturismo and droving sheep nearby*

In September 2005, Suzanne and I stayed at the **Bartoli Family's Agriturismo**, an eighteenth century farmhouse up in the mountains behind Spoleto, Umbria. A truly memorable experience: watching dramatic thunder storms from our comfortable room; walking in the nearby mountains; siestas following ample lunches of home made soup, Italian bread, local wine, Pecorino cheese made by Marcella in May; her sumptuous dinners, based on the culinary traditions of old rural families, a long communal table, and enjoyable conversations with the lively family of all ages – Suzanne acting as interpreter – and walkers from all over Europe. The warm and welcoming family farmed sheep in 1840 and still do, but would not have survived without changing their family business. In 1984 they started what became the Bartoli Agriturismo in 1988, the first in Umbria, offering riding on beautiful white horses, truffle gathering, walking, cycling, bocce bowling, a children's playground and winter excursions. Three generations work there, including 95 year-old Grandpa Domenico. Leaning on his stick, every day he watches over the farm pigs, sheep, cows, geese, ducks, cockerels and chickens and minds the vegetable garden. The Italian President's certificate acknowledges their tremendous initiative and hard work.

**Richard Adams** established **Traidcraft** in 1979. Offering the first 'alternative' and socially-oriented public share issue in the UK, it produces a wide range of fairly traded goods, including fairly traded tea. Traidcraft works with small to medium-sized enterprises throughout the developing world, providing thousands of jobs. Current sales exceed £12m per year.

**Joy Larckom** has a passion for travel and vegetables. I love her book, the *Vegetable Garden Displayed*, kept beside my bed for years. Gardening books sooth me at bedtime! Over the years, she has transformed our garden and diet. Quietly, she has achieved a revolution. Yet most people enjoying the benefits have probably never heard of her. After a year caravan touring Europe in 1976 with her husband and two children, she introduced Lollo Rosso lettuce from Italy and a range of other vegetables. She pioneered the cut-and-come-again salads we now see packed in bags in supermarkets. After a trip to China, she introduced a wide range of Chinese vegetables to British gardeners. From the USA, she brought back Oriental vegetables (Chinese, Korean, Vietnamese and Thai), which grow well in our gardens. She gave us vegetables that look good in the garden. More and more people now realise how much organic food they can grow in their back gardens, allotments or on window ledges – and give some away to neighbours. In 2004, the first time since WW2, vegetable seed sales exceeded those of flowers. (Thanks to Graham Rice for his article)

**Tim Smit** has a passionate belief in the extraordinary ability of people to achieve the impossible. In 1999, a small group of enthusiasts led by former rock star and producer, Tim, began restoring, 'on a shoestring', a once beautiful Victorian garden, the *Lost Gardens of Heligan,* which now attracts

350,000 visitors a year. He then turned a disused clay pit in Cornwall into a paradise, the equally successful *Eden Project*, enclosing Mediterranean landscapes, tropical rainforests – a 'living theatre of plants.'

*'Often, there's such a lack of understanding of what it takes to inspire people, when the only thing that motivates humans is the heart.'*

**Araki.** Suzanne and I went to the recent Barbican exhibition of the work of this pioneering Japanese photographer artist. He combines photography, painting, music and video. He loves women, old Tokyo where he was raised, and pushes boundaries and taboos. He juxtaposes love, the young, middle aged and old, death, eroticism, colours of delicious food, flowers, feminine delicacy, stark modern buildings, demolition sites, decay … extraordinary, controversial and liberating humanity, like most pioneers. At one point he used a Polaroid camera to avoid the censor.

**Dr Michael Irwin** is being investigated by the police. Retired UN medical director, head of the Voluntary Euthanasia Society, he was struck off the medical register for obtaining drugs to help a friend die. He gave advice and support to five terminally ill people to fly to Zurich's Dignitas clinic, which helps the terminally ill to die in dignity as they choose. **Anne Turner** died recently. Both are creating a proper debate about helping people exercise a choice, which is not a crime in Scotland.

**Three people I know inspire and move me. I invited them to tell their stories here. I hope they inspire you too.**

**Tree planting in Las Alpujarras.** I joined this project in November 2005. It inspired me as a model of what good work is. The Marbella coast is under severe threat from over-development. Swathes of plastic greenhouses can now be seen from space. One greenhouse spoils the scenery high in the mountains. Ancient Moorish, democratic, irrigation systems in the mountains are at risk too.

*Moorish irrigation system*

Dear Bruce,

As asked for, a potted history of our tree project: I am Trevor Taylor, for 16 years I have lived on an organic olive farm with my partner Jenny Wood in the foothills of the Sierra Nevada in southern Spain. Las Alpujarras was settled over 1,000 years ago by the Arabs of north Africa who terraced the area and set up an amazing system of irrigation, still working today. I teach Tai Chi at Cortijo Romero (C.R.), an alternative holiday/personal development centre, where I met Jordi Jutglar, a Catalan, who for many years lived at the Findhorn Foundation in Scotland, and, for 5 years was manager and general inspiration for C.R.

The owner of C.R., Alan Dale, wished to have a tree-planting project giving something back to this region, which gives so much to C.R. and its guests. Jordi and I made a proposal to run tree-planting weeks there and the Dept. of the Environment (Medio-Ambiente) granted us the use of some public land to plant and re-afforest. They loaned tools and gave us most of the trees for the project.

Our idea for the week was to plant an area in a mindful way, whilst enjoying our surroundings, ourselves and each other. We combined our talents and knowledge to create a tree-planting, meditation and Tai Chi week at C.R. and our project got under way.

We dug 500 holes, 1 metre square, by machine. The site is beside a road project which had made a real mess so it was great to think we would not only be planting trees but landscaping after the road works too.

*Jordi and Trevor*

The week was a real success. 34 people, largest group ever at C.R, came with varying ideas about what a tree-planting week was about, but mostly with an idea of giving something. With a meditation and Tai Chi (optional) before breakfast, we left for the site at 10.30am. The site was 20 minutes away by bus and on arrival we stood in a circle, held hands and Jordi led us as we listened and remembered our aims. This process helped the group focus about why we were there (i.e. mindfully planting trees, connecting with our environment, each other and ourselves).

After some safety advice regarding tools and a demonstration on how we wanted the trees planted, we worked in groups of three and planted two trees in each hole, one tree we knew would grow in this area and one experimental tree. In a few years if the experimental tree is doing well it will be the one we keep. Our idea is to give as good a start to the trees as possible. This is an arid area, so we gave each tree 5litres of water after planting.

People, left alone, got quite creative as they planted the trees and adapted our ideas. It was really interesting to see how hands-off we could be, allowing people's creativity to flourish and still maintain the ideas of the project. Control versus the individual freedom of the participants was one of the most thought-provoking observations about running such a large group. We gave people their heads and the outcome was mostly positive. With Tai Chi breaks, it became obvious that stretching was really complimentary to the work. We had picnic lunches at the site and hot soup, worked till 4.00p.m., then back to C.R. and optional sessions till 7.30 (dance, drumming, singing, meditation, etc.). We planted all the trees by Friday, had a fantastic week with

*Bruce with a fellow tree-planter*

a great sense of achievement with a group of people with all levels of skill, fitness and ages.

We ran a Spring group maintaining the site, replacing trees that had died and landscaping the area. Monitoring progress and learning from the passing of time was beneficial to the whole project and has become an integral part of our approach.

We're looking forward now to our second Spring maintenance week. As these things move on, we move on with them. Jordi and I have started an association to continue the work as an autonomous entity, El Monte Verde, while still hoping we can register under that name 'El Bosque Verde', as we want to call it, if agreed by the registration authority. The name means 'the Greenwood' which conjures up for me a natural, balanced forest eco-system. This is our dream.

'FROM LITTLE ACORNS GIANT OAKS GROW!'

Hope this is the sort of thing you were after – lots of love, Trevor

---

So far, they reckon they have planted a total of 970 trees – two species of pine, oaks, and carobs, also known as locust trees. It's beautiful! More planting: 11th to 18th November 2006 (Cortijo Romero).

**Creating Get Well UK.** Boo Armstrong inspired everyone when she shared her ideas on health and her new initiative at the BeTheChange event last Summer. I decided immediately that I'd love her story in my new book, then just a gleam in my eye. Complementary therapies have greatly benefited me. If they were accessible to everyone early enough, they could prevent unnecessary suffering and save lots of money and expensive treatments. Back, shoulder and neck pain and joint pain are the main reasons for patient referral, accounting for 55% and 17% of referrals respectively. Boo's work was recognised by the Prince of Wales's Foundation for Integrated Health when she received the new 'Integrated Health Futures Award 2005.'

*Boo Armstrong*

Dear Bruce

Fairness has always motivated me. While working at my local community health centre, I learnt about equity gaps in health care, and was particularly bothered by one – complementary therapies were being used by 20% of the UK population but 90% of these treatments were paid for privately. This meant that rich people were able to access this care and poor people could not.

Working in a poor London community, I met many people whose healthcare was affected not only by their lack of income, but also by low self-esteem, poor housing, poor diet and relationships within an often hostile society. For them, a quick visit to the doctor (8 minutes on average) and some pills didn't answer their problems. Engaging with a health professional who has the time to listen and find out exactly what is going on in this particular life often produces a diagnosis and treatment which is more specific and effective. Perhaps this is why people with money choose to buy treatment from complementary practitioners.

I wanted to do something about this inequality. Surveys show that 75% of patients want complementary therapies to be available on the NHS. 49% of GPs in England recommend them to patients, but usually without the funds to pay for their treatment. Many practitioners are well trained, insured and regulated and most importantly motivated to work with the NHS to help people in their communities to get well.

I had experience of selling health services to social services and health authorities and knew that the people commissioning services are generally fantastically busy and trying to do a good job. If I could offer them a service, which was easy to understand, covered all the areas of quality assurance and governance that it is their legal duty to comply with, and was cost effective, how could I go wrong?

In November 2000, the House of Lords published an enquiry into complementary medicine, which reported that we need more evidence and regulation in some therapies and that this medicine should be made available on the NHS with GPs acting as the gatekeepers to the service. This gave me both a mechanism to manage the flow of patients to the service and the authority with which to sell the idea.

So – after raising start-up funds and quitting my job – Get Well UK was born. We began by offering pilot services in London to find out if it works and were delighted when it did. We then borrowed a frightening amount of money via a Treasury-backed scheme, Futurebuilders-England, which gave us clout as well as finance, and proceeded to confidently share our successes and expand the service.

Our hypothesis is that we can save the NHS money through improving people's health and well-being, reducing dependency on pharmaceutical drugs and reducing patients' visits to GPs and hospitals. We also think that by valuing our health professionals and encouraging them to maintain their own wellness, everyone involved becomes more highly motivated. As Gandhi said, 'the only way to teach is by example'.

After 18 months in business, we have won two awards – the Integrated Health Futures Award and a Community Initiatives award – which I understand as recognising us as best of breed. What I hope for in the future is best in show – recognition from the wider healthcare field that what we are offering is the best medicine for many people and that our methods of providing it are second to none.

Boo Armstrong, Managing Director, Get Well UK

---

**RoadPeace** – The final contribution to this chapter is from Brigitte Chaudhry who founded RoadPeace. I became a supporter many years ago. There needs to be a complete transformation in our attitude to driving and so called road 'accidents' that cause such suffering and needless injuries and deaths. She has changed the way I drive. I am moved by her courage and determination following her personal loss and I want to help more people become aware of the work she and her supporters are doing.

---

Dear Bruce

On 27 October 1990, my only son was violently killed by a van driver who drove through red traffic lights and ploughed into Mansoor who was crossing on his motorcycle on green. He sustained terrible injuries and was declared dead two hours later. He was 26 years old, gifted and full of plans. A friend later wrote of him:

*'Mansoor was one of the most dynamic people I ever met – he was a leader, self-confident, hardworking, intelligent, almost a manic achiever...'*

We were denied access to his body, were only handed an envelope with his possessions and received no information or support. It took nine long months before we knew that five witnesses testified that the driver had also ignored the traffic that had already stopped. Yet he was only charged with 'Driving without due care and attention' and received a fine of £250 and 8 penalty points. The fact that he had killed someone was completely ignored, not even mentioned in court. This is still the legal response to the majority of culpable road deaths, for injury there is often no prosecution at all.

Mansoor Chaudhry

To this day I remain shocked and angry at the shabby and insulting treatment of my son's death, also the lack of essential information and basic human empathy suffered by our family and thousands of others.

At the time, I had no idea of the huge scale of road death and injury, since unlike other disasters, this issue was then virtually never covered in the media. Through notices in newspapers asking people to join and do something about this injustice, I received nearly 200 letters, all highlighting countless sources of suffering in addition to the loss. Some quotes illustrate these:

'I felt that our rights as parents and our son's right for justice were nowhere to be found. We were supposed to disappear in the background and not to question anything and not to expect to be given any answers...'

'As you will see, I received no support after Tony's death and none of us knew really what to do. For a family to be allowed to leave a hospital after seeing the body of their loved one in the mortuary and not being given any advice, words of consolation, a cup of tea to steady their nerves, was and still is beyond belief...'

A questionnaire I produced identified more precise areas of need and made clear that a national charity representing the interests of these traumatised people was desperately needed. The aims were to support victims, work for road danger reduction and conduct research – some bereaved and 'concerned' people joined the potential committee. In February 1992, RoadPeace was named and the first UK helpline for road victims established; in April 1993 RoadPeace received charitable status and joined FEVR, the European Federation of Road Traffic Victims.

The office was initially in my house and I answered many calls, learning much about road traffic law in practice while also bringing three judicial reviews in connection with my son's death. The more we all learnt about the law and attitudes to road danger, the clearer our campaigning aims became – proper information for victims, criminal and civil justice, national standards for crash investigation and medical treatment, and a government strategy to address this major public health and human rights issue. The second phase of our Justice Campaign (launched in 1998 and listing the above areas) is still ongoing. Part of it is a Parliamentary Group for Justice with 150 MPs and Peers. We are known as strong lobbyists for road victims' rights.

From the outset, I saw RoadPeace as a movement – against an obvious unfairness that should be of concern to all – that would be of concern if only they knew some of today's facts.

- 1.26 million people are killed on the world's roads annually – 3000 (a 9/11 disaster!) and 100,000 injured every day.
- Road traffic injury is the world's second leading cause of ill health and premature death for young men under 45.
- There is a 1 in 200 chance of dying in a road crash (UK).
- Pedestrians and cyclists account for 1 in 3 road deaths (UK).
- 25% of bereaved parents remain suicidal after 3 years (Europe).

Fourteen years of campaigning have brought only slight improvements, but there are signs that we can hope for more.

On 27 October 2005 – the 15th anniversary of Mansoor's death – I was notified by Oman's UN Ambassador in New York that the UN had just adopted the 3rd Sunday in November as the World Day of Remembrance for Road Traffic Victims – as the appropriate acknowledgement for victims of road traffic crashes and their families. RoadPeace had initiated this day in 1993 and promoted and observed it with most FEVR member organisations ever since, so we can proudly consider this our achievement. We need to build on it...

Brigitte Chaudhry, MBE, Founder & President of RoadPeace, President, European Federation of Road Traffic Victims.

---

Brigitte will soon present the road traffic victim perspective to the World Health Organisation Road Safety Collaboration Forum and relevant UN Working Parties. Because road deaths and injuries shatter lives, women around the world are at the forefront of campaigning for justice and reduction of danger on the roads. 'Women for worldwide peace on the roads' is a special campaign by RoadPeace aimed at engaging women, who have often led the call for peaceful resolutions, in a worldwide active network to bring an end to the 'war on the roads'.

*Bruce in his garden*

## Chapter 13
# Lessons from History

*'The definition of insanity is doing the same thing over and over again, and expecting different results.'*

Albert Einstein

Some nights ago, both Peter Ackroyd's *The Romantics* (BBC2) and *Battleplan* (UKTV History) set me thinking. *If only* we learned from history. Almost all the lessons we need today were there.

Reflecting as I worked in the garden, I decided to add this chapter.

**The Romantics**, from 200 years ago and more, were revolutionaries wanting liberty and justice and to create a better world.

In the middle of the eighteenth century, **Denis Diderot** – who valued *reason (head)* above all and **Jean Jacques Rousseau** – who valued *feeling (heart)* over thought, both sought to overthrow the old order in France which had the biggest police force in Europe. They united and inspired the French revolution, which went horribly wrong. **William Payne**, representing *'common sense'* carried the message of Liberty, Equality and Fraternity across the Atlantic and instigated a much more benign Declaration of Independence in 1776 and what became the United States of America. Revolutionary artist, writer and poet **William Blake**, who valued most of all the *imagination*, and represented *spirit, soul and protest*, rebelled against his traditionalist tutor, establishment Joshua Reynolds. Far ahead of his time, he wrote, *'Empire is no more'*, and barely evaded prison as a suspected dangerous subversive. He died in poverty and has only been truly recognised in the 20th and 21st Centuries. **William Wordsworth** and **Samuel Taylor Coleridge** (*The Rime of the Ancient Mariner*, dedicated to the ideals of Rousseau and Diderot) were shocked at the savage process of the French Revolution and subsequent outcomes. Narrowly escaping imprisonment as dangerous subversives, they used poetry to express their message that sanity lay in *nature and simple life*. With Blake, they were appalled at the effects of the industrial revolution, including poverty and mistreatment of children – mirrored today in the inhuman and hazardous conditions for men, women and children in some of the industrial revolution type jobs we are exporting to developing countries.

Arguably, the Romantics, together with **Freud's** discovery of the *unconscious*, and **Jung's** *collective un-conscious*, and some further lessons from history, provide us with much of what we need to guide us at the beginning of the 21st Century.

**The French Revolution** bears comparison with the Henry VIII's destructive dissolution of the monasteries and the story of idealist Oliver Cromwell's Civil War and Republic which laid waste an immense heritage and left us the poorer for it especially compared with France, Italy and Spain. There were similar patterns in the Russian Revolution, Stalin's aftermath and Mao's in China.

Oppression becomes internalised. Victims become oppressors. To every action there is a reaction.

*'Battle Plan'* reminded me that **technology wins wars**, as it did when the Moguls swept into a helpless Europe. Failure to grasp the need for a **dramatic change of strategy loses wars too**. The Japanese failed to give up their ancient tradition of individual heroism when convoys were needed. The Spanish and French experienced failures against Nelson at sea and Wellington on land. This is another way of expressing the lesson: **if you don't spot and act on a seismic change before it happens, you're 'dead'**!

Each generation has to find its own way; but the lessons of history are important.

*Jamaican family with Suzanne*

# Lessons from History

- **Most human beings just want the simple things of life**: the chance to fulfil themselves, love and family, neighbours, community, respect and dignity, basic services such as water, power, communications and transport, education and health, work that is fulfilling, sufficient income including sufficient for a decent old age.

- **This requires a society in which there is security and enough stability**, freedom from war, civil war and violence, the rule of law, freedom to express one's views and be oneself.

- **What worked in the 20th Century won't work in the 21st.** The big issues are still greed, exploitation, poverty and injustice but now the 'West' and emerging powers are in danger of destroying everything.

- **We need radical thinking**: e.g. about sustainability, debt, money, taxation and citizens' incomes.

- **Violent revolutions usually result in disappointment**, oppression and disaster. The distress of the past re-emerges in new tyrannies. Traditions may be frustrating but they help achieve stable, tolerant societies, aware of their roots, that people like to live in – e.g. London, Italy and Spain.

- **Rejoicing in diversity works better** than assimilation (compare Canada with USA and France) – the universe loves diversity.

- **The game is up for imperialism** in all its forms, commercial, national or subversive or violent regime change; unilateralism; lack of respect for other people's cultures; religious intolerance. We need universal respect.

- **'Western' domination is over**. It is also time for the new powers, all with ancient civilisations, China, India, Latin America, Islam, Africa, small nations and all the different peoples to take their place at the 'council of nations'.

- **Aggression against other countries almost always fails**. Talking and listening works. Better to put our own house in order; invest in creating a fairer society and in the poorer parts of the world – especially alleviating poverty and investing in education and health. Blockades and sanctions tend to harm the very people they are aimed to help – most often not oppressive tyrants. Constructive engagement and understanding may work best. USA, aided by Britain, traumatised a generation of young people in Iraq, and alienated Iran, the second largest source of oil and gas. USA is unwelcome in Latin America after years of imperial interference.

- **Technological superiority, so-called precision warfare, is an outdated strategy and does not offer protection**. In the 21st Century 'war' is won by hearts and minds, awareness, consciousness and community.

  *Leaders who do not understand this are dinosaurs.*

- **Virtually every people has committed dreadful atrocities**. Though we don't like to admit it, USA and Britain are no exception, both in the last 70 years, and the previous 300: all over Africa, the Caribbean, Native America, India, Australia, Vietnam, Afghanistan, the Middle East. What formed tyrants like Mugabe and Saddam? Who did they learn from?

- **We are mirrors of each other** - we see it in the other; but not ourselves.

- **Oppression and tyranny ultimately fail** - of the mind or political. It usually collapses because people rebel. So does exploitation, racism, sexism, and attempts to prevent revolutionary change.

- **Greed does not work**, brings poverty of spirit, and ultimately a revolutionary reaction.

- **'Lying', spin, denial and suppressing the truth ultimately fail**. As I write, Swiss MP Dick Marty, author of the report for the human rights watchdog, the Council of Europe, says he 'will get to the truth' about CIA 'exceptional rendering' and torture flights through European air space and refuelling despite all the obfuscation.

- **Brilliant minds are a danger** unless they have heart, spirit and balance and listen with humility, especially to people on the ground.

- **The idea of dominating nature through science has had its day**. We have to work with nature. We are part of the 'animal kingdom.' Ultimately we are dead.

- **White middle class, middle-aged men need to move over** and make way for women, black people, so-called minorities, and all human diversity and ages of people to take their proper place.

We need to embrace the words of Rabbi Michael Lerner in Ch 9, Nelson Mandela and Meg Wheatley below, and those of Rev Desmond Tutu in the next chapter, all of whom speak to our time and offer us the best inspiration for the future:

'Indeed, whether it be in the smallest community or the highest councils of nations or the world, there is a need for those simple principles according to which we have conducted our own life. These include accepting the integrity and bona fides of everyone no matter how they may differ from ourselves; loyalty no matter how much the circumstances regarding those to whom one is loyal may have changed; frankness and honesty no matter how embarrassing that may prove; and a presumption that however we may differ there are more important things we share. In other words what is required is that the mutual respect that underlies the mere possibility of negotiation should always inform the way we relate to one another as representatives of different nations and different sectors of the world community. Such a change – for it would mean some change! – would be part of building the new post-colonial global order on the international system established some 50 years ago to ensure that the world never again experienced the destructive violence of economic crisis and world war. It would be part of democratising the world in which we live. It is a necessary condition for world peace and development.'

Independent Lecture delivered by Nelson Mandela
Dublin, 12 April 2000

**'On personal courage:** One of the things that is sorely lacking in our lives is a necessary level of courage to stand up against the things we know are wrong and for the things we know are right. There are so many grievances in organisations that I think people have developed a sense of helplessness about it. And I understand that feeling of helplessness and just saying, 'I would never speak up.' But I also live with an awareness that if we don't start speaking up, we are going down a road that will only lead to increased devastation. Who was it who said, 'The only thing necessary for the triumph of evil is for good men to do nothing?' I notice that I feel powerless more than ever before. I think that's part of the tension of this time, realising that we have to lift our voices for the things we believe in, whether it's inside an organisation, or as a nation, or as a planetary community. I know that if we don't raise our voices, I can predict the future, and it's very dark.'

Meg Wheatley, *From Hero to Host*

*Mexican mountain
cattle farmer*

## Chapter 14
# There Is a Better Way

## Making sustainability mainstream – living from the heart.

> *'The earth has enough for everyone's needs,
> but not for some people's greed.'*
>
> Mahatma Gandhi

I listened, on the BBC, to John Bruton, former Irish Taoiseach, now EU Ambassador to USA. He said the USA representing only 5% of the world population, combined with the EU still representing only 13%, cannot make the rules for the world. We have to handle the re-emergence of India, China and other countries peacefully. We failed with the emergence of Germany and got ourselves into two world wars. We must not repeat these mistakes but learn from history. We have to walk with whole world.

> *'Together we can manage change; separately we run the risk of being the victims of change.'*

**We may be at a turning point.** The experience of the first few years of this

*149*

century may be forcing us to turn, as living systems do. Let us hope that dinosaur world leaders who behave like George Bush, are on the verge of extinction and the current form of globalisation is heading for extinction too! We need to release our spirits and all our creativity in making a reality of ideas like Gordon Brown's vision of free education for every child in the world.

**We have the opportunity to protect our planet** from disastrous climate change, if not too late, and ecological degradation and to create a fairer world in which every human being has a better chance of a healthy and fulfilling life. These two aspects of sustainability are inseparably linked. Such a world would be more secure and peaceful, and richer in the full meaning of the word. We would be more at ease with ourselves.

**The affluent lifestyle of that minority of people in the 'West' is at the expense of the planet and the majority of human beings living on the earth.** Right now we face environmental disaster and global injustice and poverty on a vast scale. It is a warning. These twin issues present wonderful opportunities – for learning, for increasing real wealth, or wellbeing, and self-respect. We have the opportunity to give greater meaning to our lives, rather than filling an empty hole in our hearts and comforting ourselves with constant acquisition. If we want to be happier, relative wealth and how we define it matters at least as much as absolute wealth. We do not get happier by consuming, owning or buying more. The type of society we live in contributes most to happiness.

*'All of us South Africans were less whole than we would have been without apartheid. Those who were privileged lost out as they became more uncaring, less compassionate, less humane and therefore less human; for this universe is constructed in such a way that unless we live in accordance with its moral laws, we will pay a price. Our humanity is bound together in what the Bible calls 'the bundle of life'. Our humanity is caught up in that of all others. We are human because we belong.'*

Desmond Tutu, 1999

*In the 'West' it will mean most of us giving something up, making some worthwhile sacrifices in order to regain self-respect – not charity, but fundamental change.*

**That was the message from Commonwealth leaders** at their summit in Malta, November 2005. It will mean partnership with developing and poor countries and greater respect for their cultures – rather than imposing our way, continuing exploitation, bargaining, coercing, giving with one hand, taking back with the other.

**As Vandana Shiva says**, instead of the values of appropriation, monopoly, monoculture and '**mono-thinking**,' we need values of **saving and sharing.**

Tackling climate change boldly will not so much threaten our economies as create new opportunities, new industries and new jobs and give wealthy countries like the UK the opportunity to join together with other countries as partners. Jostling for leadership is old style.

**It will require a revolution in the way we think, the words we use,** our lifestyles and the way most national and corporate leaders behave – finding common ground rather than imposing, dealing and bargaining. It will require partnership between corporations, governments, the media and advertising, NGOs, and citizens. We are all responsible and blaming others is just a 'cop out' that gets us nowhere. Sustainability in the broadest sense has to be central. It is silly to ask, as radio interviewers do all the time, *'Who's to blame?'* Blaming avoids responsibility. It is more useful to ask: *'Who is responsible?'* Of course, *'We all are.'*

*All of us must stop blaming and polarising, which are avoidance. Instead address the fundamental issues within ourselves, take responsible action and change how we live.*

**It helps to understand how nature works.** Nature is not wasteful. It recycles and reuses everything. The process is circular. Human beings are wasteful. According to the World Resources Institute, only 9% of what we spend translates into product; 90% goes into waste. Most harmful processes of our time are linear. Much of our precious waste ends up in huge and growing dumps. In waste disposal, the UK has one of the worst records in rich Europe. Many of the industrial processes and everyday products of our 21st Century high-consumption economy produce waste and toxins that nature cannot recycle.

**An outstanding example is nuclear energy**, which results in extremely dangerous waste that cannot be recycled and may take thousands of years to break down.

**We must not allow our government to take us into a new generation of nuclear power stations**, with all the unpredictable risks, costs and a thousand years of toxic waste. What if the same resources were put into the development of renewable sources like solar power? What would the benefits be to the whole world? In May 2006, Tony Blair seemed to be making an unsupported, unilateral decision to re-install a programme of building nuclear power stations. Why?

**There are lessons for us from how nature works.** In nature there is a lot of collaboration – as well as competition for territory and resources. But we have reached a stage of development where the dangers of competition are far too great and survival requires us to see ourselves as partners – with each other and all life on the planet.

A basic set of principles for ecological sustainability is the following – I have added a fourth, also observed in nature. They are totally contrary to the post-war consumer society:

**Reduce**

**Reuse**

**Recycle**

**Repair**

Following these principles, nationally and individually, would make a dramatic difference. Like our grannies' *'waste not want not.'* Interface, already mentioned, provides a prime industrial model for the world. Individuals and families can do the same.

It is natural to want to create something fresh that expresses who we are, but are we too ready to do *'out with the old and in the new?'* Victorian architecture and furniture felt oppressive but we destroyed too much. Far more Georgian and Victorian architecture was laid waste after the war than by the Luftwaffe.

**The Human Ecological Footprint** is a very useful concept. 'Footprint' is the amount of land needed to provide the resources for our current lifestyle. For example London alone currently requires over 120 times its own area – roughly equivalent to the entire productive land area of the UK – just to supply it with food. To meet all London's needs requires 293 times its geographical area (roughly twice the size of the UK). With a population of 7.4 million people, this represents 6.63 global hectares (gha) per London resident.

**If everyone on the planet were entitled to an equal share** of the Earth's bioproductive resources (termed the *average earthshare*) then we would all have 2.18 gha. This makes it clear just how unsustainable Londoners' lifestyles are. If everyone in the world were to consume as much as we do, then we would require at least three planets! (Mayor of London's Sustainable Development Website) The same kind of arguments would apply to the whole of the 'West', which is why some extreme people are thinking in terms of using other planets or space to meet our growing needs. Add to this the recent estimates that a sustainable population for the planet would be around about half the current population of six billion, moving towards eight or nine by 2050. (Professor Chris Rapley's *Green Room* on BBC News).

**Population growth is an issue**, although some people may prefer to avoid it as potentially racist. Population changes go hand in hand with poverty. It has risen from 3bn in the 1960s to 6.5bn today. Some experts predict it will rise to 9bn by 2050. Population in Russia and Old Europe is declining, except in UK, where it has risen to 60m. Immigrants are attracted to our relatively open, friendly attitude to other cultures and policy of diversity rather than assimilation. Some experts say about 2.5bn is a sustainable figure.

**Population is also misunderstood**. It is influenced by demographic breakdown. Current figures reflect the fact that India, African and South American countries have very young populations; 26% of Brazil's population is under 15 yrs. When population predictions are made, these figures are used with current birth rates to extrapolate. Unpredictable external forces may not be taken into account. The main factors are:

1 **Women's role.** Women who become emancipated and enfranchised have fewer children and start families later on in life.

2 **Health care.** Improvements in health care/water quality etc in the late 20th century led to a large young population as child mortality declined.

3 **Disease, famine, epidemics, pestilence, weather, war and civil war have the opposite effect.** HIV/AIDS is having a major impact on population in many countries especially African. By 2010, the populations of five countries – Botswana, Mozambique, Lesotho, Swaziland and South Africa – will have started to shrink because of the number dying from AIDS. In Zimbabwe and Namibia, the population growth rate will have slowed almost to zero (Avert.Org).

In the 14th Century a French sailor set foot in Weymouth. As a result, Black Death wiped out a third of Britain's population.

All of these factors mitigate population growth (New Scientist). Nevertheless, unless things fundamentally change, like consuming less of everything and eating much less meat, we shall need several times the Earth's potential resources.

**Creating Sustainable Cities** – The Sustainable City is one of the most exciting and important concepts for the new century. Whilst some of us are seeking a better life in the country, the majority are flooding into cities as they have done for centuries. In 1900 only 14% lived in large cities. By 2000 47% of the world's 6 billion humans lived in them. If this trend continues, city population will double every 38 years. There are 20 Mega-cities with populations of more than 10 million. Large cities and current construction methods present huge pollution and sustainability problems.

Mega cities have enormous footprints, as did London as early as in Victorian times, using a vast empire covering one third of the planet.

**Originally, cities like London were more self-sufficient,** with sources of food and materials within them or nearby, like Islington's long gone market gardens. Recycling was a huge business – see Dickens' *'Bleak House.'* The Victorians recycled their 'night soil' for market gardens; every scrap of timber from the fighting *'Temeraire'* battle ship was carefully recycled – look at the oak panels in Liberty's of Regent Street to see.

**A missed opportunity.** In 1858 the sewage pollution of London's 'great stink' was so bad that it halted debates in the House of Commons.

Something had to be done about the stench and the threat to health. Justus Liebig proposed a system that would reclaim the precious plant nutrients and restore them to the land - nitrogen, potash, phosphate, magnesium and calcium. His scheme was discarded in favour of Joseph Bazalgette's solution, which was to pour human waste into the Sea which is what most cities do to this day. However Berlin chose the wiser solution, which operated for about 100 years until 1985 when it was abandoned because of contamination from industrial uses. Today the technology has been mastered and the way forward is to extract the precious water **and** return the nutrients of urban sewage to the land. Already there are pioneer schemes, eg Wessex Water in UK and those of Ocean Arks in USA. It needs to be universal practice throughout the world. (Girardet, H, 2004).

**The growth of sprawling, dehumanising, unsustainable cities has been facilitated by our love affair with the motorcar.** We could not have known at the time, but this has turned out to be a disaster. Many parts of these landscapes are alien to a healthy spirit and the scale and cost of illness, crime and violence is hardly surprising. Almost all technology is a mixed blessing, except perhaps the simplest, like the bicycle. Before this, communities were a more comfortable human size, like Totnes in Devon, beautiful Spoleto in Umbria or Lucca in Tuscany.

**We now know that rampant new construction and modern redevelopment make fortunes**, but have enormous adverse effects on the environment and consume vast quantities of irreplaceable resources. Re-use, conversion and smaller scale make far better sense.

**Many Utopian, sixties redevelopments**, created with the highest hopes, often turned out to be hell to live in. Many involved large-scale demolition of pre WW1 high streets and housing. Many towns and cities emerged organically over the centuries often producing a charming variety of styles. After WW2 much redevelopment was on a bigger scale than ever before and were not constructed by craftsmen using natural materials. Such developments can be alienating, extremely expensive to put up and to demolish, both of which cause huge pollution. Also, unlike their predecessors, they may be inflexible and not easily adapted to changing needs, and soon need to be demolished. Now older houses and streets are prized. That may be the key to the future. Again, small is beautiful.

**Yet we are still doing it ... Save Britain's Heritage, the *Victorian* and residents** are campaigning against the mass demolition of good, flexible terraced housing. Under the Deputy Prime Minister's Housing Market Renewal Initiative, up to 168,000 homes will be demolished by 2016. It is almost unbelievable that we have not learned after 50 years experience. If you want to stop this unsustainable action, support Save Britain's Heritage (SAVE) and support residents campaigning against the demolition of their homes (Fight for our homes; *Victorian* journal articles).

*Berkhamsted High Street*

**Herbert Girardet is advising China** on creating its first modern, sustainable city, Dongtan (as mentioned in Chapter 2). He cites ten main factors leading to rampant urban growth: national economic development, urban accumulation of political and financial power, import substitution, economic globalisation, access to global food resources, technological development, cheap energy, expansion of urban transport systems, migration from rural areas and reproduction of urban populations. Today the consequences can be a mixed blessing, as they were in Dickens' time – some dire for people and planet.

In his short, very easily read book (Girardet, H, 1999), he describes his vision of how to bring about reconciliation between cities, their people and nature.

---

**Creating Cities for Humans**

✔ Involve the whole person - mind, spirit and body.

✔ Place long term stewardship above short term satisfaction.

✔ Ensure justice and fairness informed by civic responsibility.

✔ Identify the appropriate scale of viable human activities.

✔ Encourage diversity within the unity of a given community.

✔ Develop the precautionary principles, anticipating the effects of our actions.

✔ Ensure that our use of resources does not diminish the living environment.

---

Adapted from Girardet, H, 1999, *Creating Sustainable Cities*
Schumacher Briefings Green Books, Totnes, Devon. 1999.

Here is an abbreviated vision for the future from Richard Rogers (Rogers, R 1998, *Cities for a Small Planet*, Faber and Faber 1998).

---

**The Sustainable City**

✔ A Just City

✔ A Beautiful City

✔ A Creative City

✔ An Ecological City

✔ A City of Easy Contact and Mobility

✔ A Compact and Polycentric City

✔ A Diverse City

---

These two books are 'must reads' for civic and national leaders and anyone who considers themselves a citizen.

*Organoponicos at a home for the elderly in Havana*

If we create cities like this, sustainably, we will save billions, save the planet, save angst, social costs, disorder and ill-health, and *un-health* services and policing. When I was a young person, I dreamed of living in that kind of city. It is more possible today and as much needed.

**Kevin McCloud plans another Channel 4 series** exposing the generally poor architecture, sustainability, value and primitive construction of Britain's new 'Noddy Homes.' He wants to demonstrate that it is possible to make affordable, sustainable housing of exemplary architectural standards; *'housing that is enriching and beautifully well-built as well as affordable'* which you see in other countries. (*Observer* 27-2-06)

**Personal carbon allowances.** To stabilise $CO_2$ levels, we all need to spend less at the planet's carbon bank. This simple, practical idea is to give each of us the same allowance, held on a card like a credit/bit card, which would be swiped every time you buy petrol, an airline ticket or pay your electricity bill. Mayer Hillman and Tina Fawcett (Oxford University's Environmental Change Institute), have distilled their fears into a rather neat and practical idea. It could dramatically reduce personal $CO_2$ emissions, making the crucial targets achievable, and would also promote social equity: If you use less than your fair share, you could sell your surplus. Another route is to manage your own carbon weight, now 11 tonnes per person pa in the UK, and 20 tonnes in the US (Energy Saving Trust for tips).

**Another idea:** In the 1980s, Jacques Cousteau and his associates, Professor Lucien Malavard and Dr Bertrand Charrier looked again at wind power as a means of powering or part powering ships and developed the 'turbosail' ship. Anton Lettnor's 'Rotorship' designed on similar principles sailed across the Atlantic into New York harbour in 1926 but the idea was not taken up. Maybe the time has come to re-examine such ideas.

**One more:** I keep imagining sustainable supermarket buildings are hosts to local traders – like the amazing Victorian central market building my Dad took me to in Liverpool or its equivalent in Alamos, Mexico!

*Market building in Alamos, Mexico*

**We are all responsible.** To change things dramatically – and that is what is urgently needed – we need partnership – between business, large and small, financial markets, government and other institutions in all forms – community, local, regional, national and global – political parties, NGOs, special interest groups, the media and advertising and ordinary citizens.

**Large institutions, like government, have a tendency to exist mainly for themselves and their leaders.** They tend to deny and be inherently slow to change, conservative and cautious. Government leaders have their eye on opinion polls, their financial supporters and the next election. Likewise, large corporations exist mainly for themselves and their shareholders. Both suffer 'group think.' Both need pressure from ordinary citizens and consumers.

**Governments need to take far bolder action** and set the long-term policy frameworks for business to respond to with investment. State or regional government can put pressure on tardy national government and global institutions. A good example of this is proposed California legislation for auto manufacture, which could transform auto manufacture throughout the world.

**Government targets,** even to reduce $CO_2$ emissions by 60% by 2050 look unachievable, given our addiction to foreign travel, fossil fuel energy and imported food. Current UK air passenger numbers stand at around 180 million, up from 51 million in 1993, and projected to rise to 475 million by 2030. This would, in effect, cancel out any positives in other areas, as we go soaring past those reduction targets. Airport expansion is 'a no-brainer' as Lucy Siegle said recently in the *Observer*.

## Here are ways forward

Starting over the page are some real ideas – positive and practical ideas – that we can study and implement to start to save ourselves and the world before it is too late. They fall into two broad categories:

1) strategic priorities
2) actions for individuals like you and me.

# Strategic priorities for global and regional institutions, governments and BigCo.

## ---- *Global and Regional* ----

☑ **Reform global institutions**: especially so that small countries are properly represented and policies are for people, rather than dominated by large corporations and super rich individuals

☑ **Give support to the UN** – to resolve conflicts – especially likely in future to be over resources; prevent unilateral offensive war; resolve the causes of and outlaw 'terrorism'; bring about universal nuclear disarmament, detection and control of weapons of mass destruction; implement universal human rights; gain the support of all nations for the International Court of Justice and the International Criminal Court; achieve the Millennium Development Goals.

☑ **Make trade and social justice the key criteria for foreign policy.** Not transparently dishonest rhetoric but for real.

☑ **Prioritise support of small, poor countries** that cannot easily compete – especially fair trade, education, health and sustainable infrastructure. Eliminate obstacles to developing their economies in their own way as we did.

☑ **Support the use of Intermediate Technology for poor countries**, which is affordable for poor people, empowers them, promotes local development and has many other advantages. (Intermediate Technology Development Group – now called Practical Action)

☑ **Create a mandatory renewable operating licences** for corporations above a certain size.

☑ **Oblige companies to reduce waste** and carbon emissions and abuse of human rights.

☑ **Reform and further regulate the financial markets.**

☑ **Radically reform taxation.** Get corporations to pay their fair share of tax. Take firm action against tax havens, tax evasion, money laundering; tax speculative money transactions; introduce a 'Tobin tax'.

☑ **De-centralise energy supplies** and work towards nations, regions and areas becoming independent of non-renewable resources like oil and gas.

☑ **Turn our backs on nuclear arms and energy** – a major threat to security and safety, costly and creating a legacy of dangerous toxic waste for hundreds or thousands of years.

☑ **Instead, invest in developing a variety of renewable sources** and increase the efficiency of existing power generation and equipment to reduce carbon and other harmful emissions.

☑ **Prioritise cleaner aircraft engines and more efficient planes.**

☑ **Reduce international travel and transportation of goods by air.**

#### ---- *National* ----

☑ **Support the above.**

☑ **Take firm action to remove the obstacles for women and others who are discriminated against** to take their place at the 'top tables'.

☑ **Work towards regional and local economies** that reduce polluting transportation, congestion and concreting over our land.

☑ **Implement joined-up policies** for sustainability in the broadest sense. Take this out of short term politics.

☑ **Tax the unsustainable** so that people pay prices that fully reflect real costs to society and the environment.

☑ **Tax those forms of transport that are least sustainable** and contribute most to carbon emissions; give back to the most sustainable.

☑ **Invest in fast strategic railways**, connecting major cities, for freight and passenger travel. Take this out of the hands of timid and inconsistent politicians.

☑ **Minimise investment in airport expansion and motorways.**

☑ **Take strategic action to revitalise our countryside and ghost towns.**

☑ **Re-asses the values underlying education.**

☑ **Promote a culture that values food quality** – fresh and local.

☑ **'Grasp the nettle' with supermarkets and similar national multi-scale retailers.** Require them to provide industry agreements or impose renewable charters. Create a regulator and measures to protect small retailers and suppliers. The nation's health and the planet depend on it.

☑ **Cut expenditure on defence, war and supplying arms to poor countries** – get out of the arms trade.

☑ **Enable citizens to withdraw from taxation attributable to warfare.**

☑ **UK penal reform.** Like the USA, we lock up more people than any other country in Europe – at great expense. Investing in sustainable communities, prevention, remedial care and rehabilitation instead of locking people up and mistreating them, including women, young people and children, would save a lot of money and wasted lives.

## ---- *National and Local* - with the money saved ----

☑ **Increase expenditure on effective programmes** to help poor countries, especially remembering those that made Britain rich.

☑ **Give local authorities and communities the autonomy needed to create sustainable cities, towns and communities.**

☑ **Subsidise those forms of transport that contribute the least $CO_2$** - like trains, clean energy buses, walking and cycling.

☑ **Subsidise the development of a wide variety of renewable, preferably local, energy sources and energy re-use.**

☑ **Recycle human sewage** - promote extraction technology that extracts the water and restores the nutrients to the land.

☑ **Plan land use** - in partnership with developers and businesses and all stakeholders. Design new developments with good public transport and a wide range of local services to reduce the need to travel.

☑ **Encourage local food and energy self-sufficiency.**

☑ **Encourage small, organic farmers** and cap support for larger farmers

☑ **Make it a strategic Sustainability Policy priority to support small shops on the high street.**

☑ **Provide a basic citizens' income and decent citizens' pensions,** not based on contributions - and save even more. Both will ultimately save enormous social and bureaucratic costs and expenditure on other services resulting from alienation, wasted talent and poverty!

☑ **Provide free education and health (rather than ill health) services**

☑ **Spend more on universities**, research and make university education free.

☑ **Provide extra help for deprived communities.**

**And now for you and me:**

Homes account for around one third of total $CO_2$ emissions in UK.

# ---- *Actions for individuals like you and me* ----

## Saving the planet and creating a fairer world

Homes account for around one third of total $CO_2$ emissions in UK.

*Bruce's garden with vegetables and flowers*

☑ **Reduce, Reuse, Recycle and Repair**

☑ **Be content with less.**

☑ **Become a global, citizen activist.** Think about the majority in the world, here and elsewhere. Recognise when you have no real understanding of countries and learn! Lobby your politicians; lobby global institutions and big corporations; join campaigns; support NGOs; get out on the streets if necessary.

☑ **Challenge Government, EU and Global regulations and policies.** Some are sustainable and promote global justice – others do the exact opposite – many are just not bold enough. Be watchful and lobby hard with your representatives. You can easily spot when politicians and business people obfuscate and are in denial.

☑ **Use your purchasing power to change your world.** Choose what you want to encourage; buy organic, GM free and fair trade; examine where things come from, consider the food miles, how they got here, how they were produced, how workers were treated. Avoid products and companies that do harm, and packaging that cannot be recycled. Lobby retailers.

☑ **If necessary, pay more to live by your values.**

☑ **Choose an ethical bank or building society**, affinity credit cards that reflect your values and ethical investments.

☑ **Calculate your annual personal carbon emissions** – reduce and ration yourself. (Hillman, M)

☑ **Turn off appliances** – one billion computers on standby produce a lot of $CO_2$.

☑ **Buy and shop locally** – often cheaper if you take everything into account; rather than drive, get stuff delivered.

☑ **Generally eat within the seasons.**

☑ **Grow at least some of your vegetables.** Gardening, working with your hands, gives you exercise and, done with mindfulness, is meditation.

☑ **Drink tap, not bottled, water** where it is safe.

☑ **Compost anything that will decompose** (taking precautions against attracting rats): fruit and vegetables, clippings, leaves, screwed up or torn up cardboard. Leave your grass cuttings on the lawn. Get advice (HDRA).

☑ **Make your garden friendly to wildlife**; not too tidy, leave seed heads and berries over winter. Throw out leftovers like stale breadcrumbs for the birds.

☑ **Grow hedges where possible.** Hedges, unlike fences, harbour life and last forever. Don't use wood, steel or materials that need treating.

☑ **Manual work is good for you.** Winston Churchill knew, building his wall. Use hand rather than power tools – within reason. Use shears and a hand mower – less noise and other pollution; better for your muscles, the environment, your pocket – no need to drive to the sports centre to keep fit.

- ☑ **Don't turn your front garden into a car park.**

- ☑ **Give up eating a lot of meat** – methane gas and the grain-to-meat ratio is unsustainable – make sure it is organic or wild.

- ☑ **Consider how the animals** involved in your food, pharmaceutical or beauty products are treated.

- ☑ **Conserve water.**

- ☑ **Save wood** – conserve and plant trees.

- ☑ **Check wooden furniture is from a sustainable source**; better still buy second hand.

- ☑ **Think before you drive or fly**; walk, cycle – if you dare – or use train or bus. Flying accounts for 11% of UK harmful $CO_2$ emissions. Fly less and plant trees to make up for emissions. Flying in cheap seats, or in the likes of EasyJet does less harm.

- ☑ **Drive the most eco-friendly vehicle** you can – get rid of 4-wheel drive vehicles (unless you work on the land), SUVs, MPVs, gas guzzlers; keep to the speed limits.

- ☑ **No patio heaters!** – a symbol of what we have to give up!

- ☑ **Consider a car club**, or could you manage with one car?

- ☑ **Make your home eco-friendly and energy efficient.**

- ☑ **Use sustainable appliances**, white ware, DIY and garden tools – hand in preference – and switch things off.

- ☑ **Avoid toxic DIY products and non-renewable materials** – e.g. toxic paints, UPVC windows. Repair wooden windows; get advice from CAT or FOE.

- ☑ **Look again at how our grannies managed the home and how they cleaned things.**

- ☑ **Minimise use of plastic** – e.g. packaging – and reuse or recycle when you can.

- ☑ **Slow down** and do one thing at a time when possible.

☑ **Follow your heart**, know yourself and live in a way that reflects your values.

☑ **Be gentle with yourself** and available for those you love.

*'Activism is my rent for living on the planet.'*

Alice Walker

I take a hopeful view that living systems work benignly on balance. It is the story of human history. We have not destroyed ourselves. Transformation will happen whatever we do. It is our opportunity to choose to influence it for the better.

**The final challenge is to everyone:** realise we are *all* leaders and can take our power in changing our world. Whatever you do, no matter how insignificant it may feel, is important. Discover your 'core purpose' – why you are here. Follow your heart! Your passion will be your source of energy.

For everyone, a useful question is:

*'What is it that the world of tomorrow needs,*
*that I am uniquely able to provide?'*

Dr Peter Hawkins
Chairman, Bath Consultancy Group

To *'the world of tomorrow,'* I add *'the world of today.'*

*Two young people off to see the world – a park in Seville*

BCN – 2nd June, 2006

# Resources and References

**Car clubs** – How to get started: Streetcar, 08456 448 476, www.streetcar.co.uk

**CarPlus**, 0113-234 9299; www.carplus.org.uk. The CarPlus website has a database of car clubs around the country, as well as details of lift-sharing, a scheme for sharing the use of private cars. For the Department for Transport's guidance for residential and workplace travel planning see: www.dft.gov.uk/stellent/groups/dft_susttravel/documents/divisionhomepage/031341.hcsp.

DfT's 2004 report *'Smarter Choices: Changing the Way We Travel'* includes studies of car clubs in Edinburgh and Bristol; see www.dft.gov.uk/stellent/groups/dft_susttravel/documents/divisionhomepage/031340.hcsp

**Money, taxation and citizens' incomes and pensions** see James Robertson's website www.jamesrobertson.com

Robertson, J & Bunzl, J, 2003, *Monetary Reform – Making it Happen!* International Simultaneous Policy Organisation (ISPO)

For an Islamic view of debt money see El Diwany, T, 2003, *The Problem with Interest*, Kreatoc Ltd

Shakespeare R & Challen, P, 2002, *Seven Steps to Justice*, New European Publications

Madron, R & Jopling, J, 2003, *Gaian Democracies*, Schumacher Briefings, Green Books.

Tax Justice Network, www.taxjustice.net

## Sources for Practical Advice or Action

- Centre for Alternative Technology, www.cat.org.uk
- *Change the world for a fiver, We are what we do*, 2004, Short Books, London www.wearewhatwedo.org
- Energy Saving Trust, www.est.org.uk
- Friends of the Earth, www.foe.co.uk
- GM Freeze, www.gmfreeze.org
- Henry Doubleday Research Association, leading EU centre for organic cultivation advice, heritage and organic seeds and plants now renamed Garden Organic, www.hdra.org.uk
- Hillman, M, 2004, *How We Can Save the Planet*, Penguin
- *No waste like home*, Virgin Books, London.
- Oakley, C, 2004, *52 Ways to change your world*, Centre for Alternative Technology
- Patel, S, ed, 2005, *The little book of big ideas*, Friends of the Earth, Think-Books, London
- Poyzer, P and Hickman, L, 2005, *A Good Life*, Eden Project Books, London.

- Simply Switch, www.simplyswitch.com makes it easy to switch
- Smith, A and Baird, N, 2005, *Save Cash & Save the Planet*, Collins
- WriteToThem.com, http://www.writetothem.com/write

## World Resources Institute

www.wri.org. a newsroom of enlightened action. Their mission is to move human society to live in ways that protect Earth's environment for current and future generations by using knowledge to catalyze public and private action to:

**Reverse damage to ecosystems.** Protect the capacity of ecosystems to sustain life and prosperity.

**Expand participation in environmental decisions.** Collaborate with partners worldwide to increase people's access to information and influence over decisions about natural resources.

**Avert dangerous climate change.** Promote public and private action to ensure a safe climate and sound world economy.

**Increase prosperity while improving the environment.** Challenge the private sector to grow by improving environmental and community wellbeing.

## General references and resources

- ActionAid, www.actionaid.org.uk
- AddAction, www.addaction.org.uk
- Agriturismo, www.agriturismobartoli.it ; www.agriturismo.com ; www.agriturismo.net
- Alcohol Concern, www.alcoholconcern.org
- Alex Skibinsky, a.skibinski@ntlworld.com
- Alternative Energy, www.bpalternativenergy.com
- Alternet – America's debt time bomb, http://www.alternet.org/story/28646/
- Amnesty International, www.amnesty.org
- Anti-Slavery International, www.antislavery.org
- Apollo Alliance, www.apolloalliance.org
- ASH, www.ash.org.uk
- Bad Buildings, http://www.badbuildings.co.uk
- Bartoli Family's Agriturismo, www.agritourismobartoli.it
- BBC Jennifer Chevalier, 11-1-2006, BBCNews.co.uk
- BBC World Service Trust.org www.bbc.co.uk/worldservice/trust
- BedZed, www.bedzed.org.uk

- BeTheChange, www.bethechange.org.uk
- Building Research Establishment Environmental Assessment Method (BREEAM), www.breeam.org
- CAFOD, www.cafod.org.uk
- Capra, F, 2002, *The Hidden Connections – A Science for Sustainable Living*, Harper Collins, London.
- Carlo Petrini, *the Slow Revolutionary*, www.time.com/time/europe/hero2004/petrini.html
- Castro, F, 1993, *Tomorrow is Too Late, Development and the environmental crisis in the Third World*, Ocean Press, Melbourne.
- Centre for Citizen Media, citmedia.org
- Centre for Tomorrow's Company, www.tomorrowscompany.com
- Charter 88, www.charter88.org.uk
- Chris Cook, www.althousing.net/chriscook.html
- Chris Cook's Asset Based Finance, www.opencapital.net
- Chris Rapley's Green Room, BBC News, news.bbc.co.uk/2/hi/science/nature/4585920.stm
- Christian Aid, www.christianaid.org
- Christian Council for Monetary Justice, www.ccmj.org
- Collins J. and Porras J, 1996, *Built to Last – The Habits of Visionary Companies*, Harvard Business School Press, USA.
- Conscience, www.conscienceonline.org.uk
- Corporate Watch, www.corpwatch.org
- Cortijo Romero, www.cortijo-romero.co.uk 01494 765775 Cortijo Romero, Cottage Offices, Latimer Park, Latimer Road, Chesham, HP5 1TU
- Country Markets – formerly WI Markets, www.country-markets.co.uk
- Creating Better Workplaces for the 21st Century, www.brucenixon.com
- Cuba Organic Support Group, www.cosg.org.uk
- Cuba Si, www.cuba-solidarity.org
- Cultural Creatives, www.culturalcreatives.org
- Curtis, M, Unpeople – *Britain's Secret Human Rights Abuses*, 2004 and *Web of Deceit – Britain's Real Role in the World*, 2003, Vintage, UK
- Curtis, M, *Unpeople – Britain's Secret Human Rights Abuses*, Vintage, UK.
- Dowden, R, Director of the Royal Africa Society, The Africa Issue, *Independent* 1-6-2005.
- Earth Policy Institute, www.earth-policy.org

- Ecologist, www.theecologist.org
- El Diwany, T, 2003, *The Problem with Interest,* Kreatoc Ltd, London, www.islamic-finance.com/indexnew.
- Electoral Reform Society, www.electoral-reform.org.uk
- Enterprising Britain, www.sbs.gov.uk/enterprisingbritain
- Equal Opportunities Commission, www.eoc.org.uk
- *Ethical Corporation* magazine, www.ethicalcorp.com
- Ethical Performance, www.ethicalperformance.com
- *FastCompany*, issue 96 July 2005, www.fastcompany.com/magazine/96
- Fax your MP and MEP, www.FaxYourMP.com
- Fight for our homes, www.fightforourhomes.com
- Foodaware, www.foodaware.org.uk
- Fonda, J, Speech at the National Women's Leadership Summit, June, 2003, www.thewhitehouseproject.org/whp_news/update_June_2003.htm
- Get Well UK, www.getwelluk.com
- Girardet, H, 1999, *Creating Sustainable Cities*, Schumacher Briefings, Green Books, Totnes, Devon
- Girardet, H, 2004, *CitiesPeoplePlanet – Liveable Cities for a Sustainable World*, Wiley-Academy
- Global Justice Movement, www.globaljusticemovement.net
- GM Update Campaign, www.soilassociation.org
- GM Freeze, www.gmfreeze.org
- Graham Rice's profile of Joy Larkom http://grahamrice.com/currently/yourgarden/0501joy.html
- Green Alliance, www.green-alliance.org.uk
- Green Business, www.greenbusines.net
- Green Car Congress, www.greencarcongress.com
- Greenpeace, www.greenpeace.org
- Greenleaf Servant Leadership, www.greenleaf.org  and www.servantleadership.org.uk
- *Havana Journal* http://havanajournal.com/business_comments/A1415_0_4_0_M/ I
- Hawkins P, 2006, *The Wise Fool's Guide to Leadership*, O Books.
- Institute for Public Policy Research, www.ippr.org.uk
- Interface, www.interfaceinc.com

- Intermediate Technology Development Group (now called Practical Resources) The Schumacher Centre for Technology & Development, www.itdg.org – aims to demonstrate and advocate the sustainable use of technology to reduce poverty in developing countries.
- International Action Center (IAC), www.iacenter.org
- James Robertson – Working for a sane alternative www.jamesrobertson.com
- Jamie Oliver, www.jamieoliver.net and www.channel4.com/schooldinners
- Jane Fonda, www.awakenedwoman.com/jane_fonda_talk.htm
- Japan for Sustainability, a not-for-profit organisation with aims to communicate to the world the steps that are being made towards sustainability in Japan. http://www.japanfs.org/en/newsletter/200510.html
- Jeanine de Waele, Artist, www.jeaninedewaele.co.uk
- Job Ownership Limited, JOL, www.jobownership.co
- John Ince is the producer/director of a new documentary about America's debt crisis. For more information, visit TIME-BOMB.org.
- Joseph Stiglitz, http://www.infid.be/hypocrisy_imf.html
- Jubilee 2000, www.jubilee2000uk.org
- Jubilee Research, www.jubileeresearch.org/latest/debtrelief0605.htm
- *Lancet*, www.thelancet.com
- Leggett, J, 2006, *Half Gone: Oil, Gas, Hot Air and the Global Energy Crisis*, Portobello Books. Independent Books Direct on 08700 798 897
- Liz Ryan, *Time*, November 2003, lizryan@worldwit.org
- Local Works, www.localworks.org
- Lohas, www.lohas.com
- London Hydrogen Partnership, www.lhp.org.uk
- LSE, http://www.lse.ac.uk
- Lovelock, J, 2006, *The Revenge of Gaia, Why the Earth Is Fighting Back – and How We Can Still Save Humanity*, Allen Lane.
- Madron, R and Jopling, J, 2003, *Gaian Democracies – redefining globalisation and people-power,* Green Books for the Schumacher Society, www.wdm.org.uk
- Mayor of London's Sustainable Development Website www.citylimitslondon.com and www.london.gov.uk/mayor/sustainable-development/susdevcomm_footprint.jsp
- Michael Moore, www.michaelmoore.com
- Millennium Campaign, www.millenniumcampaign.org
- Monbiot, G, 2001, *Captive State – The Corporate Takeover of Britain*, Pan Books, London

- National Economic and Social Rights Initiative. www.nesri.org/media_updates
- National Priorities Organisation www.nationalpriorities.org
- New Consumer www.newconsumer.org
- New Economics Foundation (NEF), Mirage and Oasis, www.neweconomics.org and Wellbeing Programme www.neweconomics.org/gen/well-being_current.aspx
- New Politics Network www.new-politics.net
- New Scientist www.newscientist.com/article/mg15921429.300.html
- Nonviolent Communication www.nonviolentcommunication.com
- OneWorld.net November 30, 2005, www.oneworld.net
- Open Space – Harrison Owen www.openspaceworld.org
- Oxfam www.oxfam.org
- Oxford Council on Good Governance (OCGG) www.oxfordgovernance.org
- Peace Pledge Union, www.ppu.org.uk
- Polarity management, www.polaritymanagement.com
- Policy Studies Institute, www.psi.org.uk
- Political Affairs Magazine, www.politicalaffairs.net/article/view/1615/1/112
- Porritt, J, 2005, *Capitalism As If The World Matters*, Earthscan.
- Positive News, www.positivenews.com
- Power to the People, www.powerinquiry.org
- Practice of Peace, www.practiceofpeace.com
- Pretty JN, Lang T, Morison J, Ball AS, 2005, Food Miles and Farm Costs: the full cost of the British food basket. *Food Policy* 30(1), 1-20.
- Rabbi Michael Lerner,Tikkun Community, *A New Bottom Line,* www.tikkun.org
- Resurgence, www.resurgence.org
- Rex Cinema, www.therexcinema.com
- Richard Adams, www.newstatesman.co.uk/upstarts/2005/upstarts2005winners.htm
- RoadPeace supports road traffic victims and educates about road danger, www.roadpeace.com  brigitte.chaudhry@roadpeace.org, 020 8964 1800 Helpline, 0845 4500 355, RoadPeace receives no statutory funding; 80% of its funding comes from victims.
- Robert Greenleaf Centre for Servant-Leadership, www.greenleaf.org and www.servantleadership.org.uk
- Robertson, J and Bunzl, J, 2004, *Monetary Reform – Making it Happen!* International Simultaneous Policy Organisation, London, www.simpol.org
- Rogers, R 1998, *Cities for a Small Planet*, Faber and Faber 1998

- Rowbotham, M, 2000, *The Grip of Death, A study of modern money, debt slavery and destructive economics*, Jon Carpenter Publishing, Charlbury, Oxon, UK.
- Royal Africa Society, www.royalafricansociety.org
- Save Britain's Heritage, SAVE, www.savebritainsheritage.org
- SELF, www.self.org
- Schumacher College, www.schumachercollege.org.uk
- Schumacher Society, www.schumachersociety.org
- Shakespeare, R and Challen, P, 2002, *Seven Steps to Justice*, New European Publications and Global Justice Movement, www.globaljusticemovement.net
- Shakepeare, R and Choudhury, M A, *The Universal Paradigm*, 2006
- Shaping a Fairer Future, www.4ni.co.uk/nationalnews.asp
- Shepherd, A and Scott, N, 2005, *Reduce, Reuse, Recycle*, Green Books
- Sherwood Enterprise Village, www.sev.org.uk
- Shiva,V, *Earth Democracy – justice, sustainability and peace*, 2005, Zed Books, London.
- SiSpain, www.sispain.org/english/history/muslim
- Slow City, www.citymayors.com/environment/slow_cities
- Slow Food, www.slowfood.com
- Soil Association, www.soilassociation.org
- Sustainable Investment, www.sustainable-investment.org
- Sustainable Investment Research Institute, SIRIS, www.siris.com.au
- *The Servant Leader – From Hero to Host* – an Interview with Margaret Wheatley, The Greenleaf Centre for Servant-Leadership, 2002, www.margaretwheatley.com
- Tim Smit, who created the Lost Gardens of Heligan, www.heligan.com and the Eden Project
- Tobin Tax Initiative, www.tobintax.org
- Tutu, D, 1999, *No Future without Forgiveness*, Ryder.
- TraidCraft, www.traidcraft.org.uk
- Transport 2000, www.transport2000.org.uk
- UK Social Investment Forum, www.uksif.org
- UN Millennium Goals, www.un.org/millenniumgoals
- Vandana Shiva, www.zmag.org and her Reith Lecture www.news.bbc.co.uk/hi/english/static/events/reith_2000/lecture5.stm and www.wikipedia.org/wiki/Vandana_Shiva

- The *Victorian,* www.victoriansociety.org.uk
- Wangari Maathai, www.foe.co.uk/campaigns/biodiversity/news/wangari and www.wangarimaathai.or.ke
- WDM – World Development Movement, www.wdm.org.uk
- Weisbord, M and Janoff, S, 1995, *Future Search*, Berrett-Koehler, San Francisco
- Wheatley, M, 1994, *Leadership and the New Science – Learning about Organisation from an Orderly Universe*; 1996, *A Simpler Way*; 2002, *Turning to One Another: Simple Conversations to Restore Hope to the Future*, Berret-Koehler, San Fransisco; 2002, *The Servant Leader – From Hero to Host*, www.margaretwheatley.com
- Women for worldwide peace on the roads campaign/Women for Peace on the Roads, www.roadpeace.org
- Women in Agriculture, http://www.navdanya.org/publications/women-agri.htm
- World Development Movement, www.wdm.org.uk
- World Watch Institute, www.worldwatch.org/topics/energy/climate

# Index

# Endorsements

## Living System – making sense of sustainability

*Exciting, thought provoking, dynamic, irritating, inspiring, passionate and occasionally enraged, Bruce Nixon forces us to re-evaluate our lives. His philosophy, that of core sustainability, just might hold the key to greater happiness for us all.*
**Kevin McCloud**
Kevin McCloud, journalist, television presenter and WWF ambassador

*An excellent read – personal, immediate and accessible, based on much of the author's own multi-faceted life experience. The book is universal in its scope and aimed at each of us, our personal choices and their application in every day life. We are all hopefully essential, integral and integrated components of 'living systems'. The book is about living within Gaia's constraints and always remembering that an ounce of practice is worth a ton of theory!*
**Diana Schumacher**
Environmentalist

*This is both a very wise and a very human book. Its greatest strength is that it weaves together the radical changes needed at the global level with the changes each of us can make today in our own lives and shows how both are part of the same living system. It is passionately pro-enterprise and passionately against the abuse of corporate power. It truly shows how we can move towards an 'economics that works for people and the planet'. I endorse it in the strongest possible terms.*
**Stewart Wallis**
Executive Director, nef (the new economics foundation)

*The contest between forces of life and forces of anti-life is the epic struggle of our times. The rule of abstract notions of economic growth and globalisation is destroying life on earth. In 'Living System' Bruce Nixon takes us back to the basics of the processes that threaten life and processes that maintain and nurture life.*
**Dr Vandana Shiva**
Leading Environmentalist and Director of the Navdanya Research Foundation for Science, Technology and Ecology, India, www.navdanya.org

*This powerful book highlights the choice we face; if a minority of powerful nations continue to enforce an economic system under pinned by centralised technologies and vulnerable supply lines, they will need to protect it with a huge world wide police force at enormous expense and risk to all our civil liberties. On the other hand, if we all begin a shift to decentralised world economy based on equitable and efficient use of energy, renewable energy sources, and re-localised supply systems, we can create. communities that no terrorist organisation can easily threaten and, perhaps more importantly, which threaten no one else.*

**Paul Allen**
Development Director, Centre for Alternative Technology

*In our increasingly busy lives we should welcome anything that helps to introduce a breath of fresh air, but Bruce Nixon's book does more than this. This book demands readers take responsibility for their decisions and life choices but, in return, it highlights the potential for new outcomes that could be achieved to benefit us all.*

*It is a challenging read for those who will engage with the issues, but it also offers fresh optimism to those who recognise the opportunities of the positive future it outlines for the planet, if we dare to take the path.*

**Dr Susan Kay-Williams**
Chief Executive, Garden Organic
(formerly Henry Doubleday Research Association)

*No matter where you live - from northern industrial societies to the developing south - we are heading into a climate change crisis that will threaten food security, the management of water and sustainable energy. The globalisation agenda of big corporations just accelerates the problem. We have to have a different starting point for surviving and living differently. Bruce Nixon explores this crisis and offers a different set of choices about where we can start from and what we must do. Everyone of us needs to address the challenges he explores and begin to make the changes needed to survive....while we have time to do so.*

**Alan Simpson**
Member of Parliament, Nottingham South,
Nominated for the ITN Ecohero Award

*Bruce Nixon writes with insight, intelligence and grace, showing us that we can and must discover and act on our shared vision for a healthy, sustainable world. We all stand at the edge of the unknown, having never confronted such pace of change and growing harm to the air we breath, the water we drink and the societies we build. We can choose to nurture instead of destroy. We can choose to tolerate our differences instead of aggress against them. We can choose to come together instead of pull apart. Bruce's ideas and understandings encourage positive possibilities and that, to me, is a sign of hope and love. It is my pleasure to encourage everyone who cares, to read this book.*

**Sandra Janoff, Ph.D.,**
Co-Director, Future Search Network, Wynnewood, PA, USA

*This is not just another explanation of the problems of the world. Its ambition is to make links, provide context and, above all, promote thought and a response. If you want to be an active citizen, give it a try; it might just change the way you think about the world.*

**Benedict Southworth**
Director WDM, campaigning for justice for the world's poor.

*This book's strength is its optimism. It is not afraid to set out all the problems we face, bringing in witnesses where appropriate, and it would be easy to despair at the mountains to be climbed, but it also draws together examples of initiatives that are going in the right direction, examples of people standing up to the problems and deciding to do something different. All the examples of initiatives that are changing people's lives should persuade readers that the world does not have to be like this. An inspiring book"*

**Stephen Joseph OBE**
Executive Director Transport 2000: Putting people and the environment first - the campaign for sustainable transport.

*I really hope you will read this book. Treat it as a journey, on which you travel with Bruce Nixon to excavate and examine the foundations of our society and its ecological systems. Become angry over the injustice of poverty, alarmed at the destruction of our natural world, aware of the dilemmas that face us all and hopeful at the new renaissance that is unfolding. It is rare to find a book that is both illuminating and accessible. Read it and go on your own journey.*

**Barry Coates**
Executive Director, Oxfam New Zealand

*Bruce Nixon has compiled much interesting material both to point out the problems of today's world and to indicate where we might go from here. The challenges are vast, and only a quantum jump in problem solving will now do.*
**Herbert Girardet**
Author, consultant and filmmaker on sustainability and sustainable cities

*If you want to shift your focus from a culture of control to a culture of participation, then this powerful book will prove to be your best and invaluable companion. This is a good guide to sustainability – do not only read it but act upon it.*
**Satish Kumar**
Founder of the Small School and Director of Programmes
at Schumacher College, Editor of *Resurgence*, Devon, England.

*I warmly welcome the integrity of Living Systems. The behaviour of companies of all sizes have fundamentally changed in response to globalisation, yet at a deep spiritual level, we need to appreciate fully that we are in the universe, the universe is within us and that the universe and us are connected.*
**Dr Neslyn Watson-Druée, MBE, FRCN, D Univ, FCGI,** pioneer honoured for her work in promoting diversity in nursing

*'Ordinary people change the world' says Bruce Nixon in this challenging book. Take that seriously: be challenged: read this book.*
**Ron Bailey**
Campaign Organiser, Local Works, Campaigning for
a Local Communities Bill to empower people
to improve their local communities  www.localworks.org

*This book is very easy to browse through. Anyone who reads it will be enlightened by its contents and feel encouraged to make that extra effort towards changing our wasteful and materialistic culture into a sustainable one. Many examples in the book show how just one person can make a huge difference in changing the thinking of our wasteful and materialistic culture into a sustainable one. A pebble dropped into a pool will cause the water to ripple outwards, so too can each person through their actions contribute to this growing movement of ecologically minded human beings.*
**Robin Joffre**
Mother, grandmother, sister, friend
and concerned citizen of the earth, Montreal

*Bruce Nixon's 'Living System – Making Sense of Sustainability' puts humanity's priorities in the right perspective as the processes of globalisation unfold. It is a mine of useful information for those concerned to ensure the preservation of lasting human values and the security of the environment in a world, which is threatening to self-destruct morally and materially.*
**Dr Ian McDonald**
Chief Executive Officer of the Sugar Association of the Caribbean, Georgetown, Guyana

*I warmly recommend this book and its systemic approach. Among its other merits, it brings out clearly that the present money system is systematically structured to produce perverse outcomes; and why systematic restructuring, national and international, of taxation, public spending, the creation of money, etc – based on sharing the value of common resources more fairly – is needed to produce more benign and sustainable outcomes across the whole range of human activity.*
**James Robertson**
Working for a Sane Alternative, Oxfordshire, England.

*Bruce Nixon has written a short but challenging book for business. He identifies the need to change what motivates and drives business forward as something that has to happen quickly and shows by examples how putting people and the planet first can also work for business. He rightly identifies the desire to dominate nature as an attitude that belongs to a previous era and GM crops as, hopefully, the last step up the ladder of intensification of farming which has already destroyed so much of the planet's biodiversity and beauty.*
**Pete Riley**
Campaigns Director, GM Freeze

*It's no longer a question of whether we recognise the threat of climate change, it's what we now do about it - collectively and individually. Just as the Environmental Audit Select Committee is set up to investigating how well sustainable development policy is integrated into government policy, so this book challenges individuals to scrutinise their own stance and their own action. The challenge of climate change is here and doing nothing is not an option. It's about what we can do.*
**Joan Walley, MP**
Parliamentary Environmental Audit Select Committee

*Bruce Nixon is to be congratulated on this tour de force of enlightened and provocative thinking on the pros and cons of globalisation, especially with regard to the dangers to small, poor, developing states, of unfettered trade in goods and services, with the rules skewed unfairly in favour of the rich and powerful. He writes with passion and commitment to cajole, persuade and convince that we, individually and collectively, have it within ourselves to effect change and to make all that we do sustainable.*

**Dr Riyad Insanally**
Senior Trade Adviser, Guyana High Commission, London

*Reading this excellent study and its huge range of sensibly ordered research, it grew and grew upon me. I realised how delicately and bravely the author was being sensitive to where people are, acknowledging the reality of denial, and yet unfolding a massive challenge. We are all bound to start where we are, but now it needs be with a profound change of perception. This book provides it. It identifies committed hope emergent in the Global scene and aids the ability to deal with the extreme urgency of effecting root and branch change in our economic behaviour.*

**Canon Peter Challen**
Chairman of the Christian Council for Monetary Justice, London

*This extraordinary and invaluable book offers an original approach and fresh insights to a subject that is now, rightly, attracting so much attention. It is painstaking in its portrayal of the systemic problems facing the planet, and clear about the implications that these present to us. This is a profoundly optimistic work, an affirmation of the good in people and their ability to heal the system. In essence it is a call for personal transformation, a comprehensive explanation as to why it is so imperative, and a tantalising vision of how different everything could look in the brave new world that would emerge.*

**John Noble**
Director of the Greenleaf Centre for Servant-Leadership UK, London.